Ian Morris read medicine and then philosophy and logic at Cambridge. Whilst training in surgery he spent some time in medical research. He worked as a hospital doctor in Yorkshire. He is a Methodist local preacher and has used his experience in scientific and philosophical thinking to study the origins of the Gospels.

Ian is married with two children and two grandchildren.

Ian Morris

WRITTEN FOR FAITH

St John's Gospel:
A true witness?

AUSTIN MACAULEY PUBLISHERS™
LONDON • CAMBRIDGE • NEW YORK • SHARJAH

Copyright © Ian Morris (2021)

The right of Ian Morris to be identified as author of this work has been asserted by the author in accordance with section 77 and 78 of the Copyright, Designs and Patents Act 1988.

All rights reserved. No part of this publication may be reproduced, stored in a retrieval system, or transmitted in any form or by any means, electronic, mechanical, photocopying, recording, or otherwise, without the prior permission of the publishers.

Any person who commits any unauthorized act in relation to this publication may be liable to criminal prosecution and civil claims for damages.

A CIP catalogue record for this title is available from the British Library.

ISBN 9781398413535 (Paperback)
ISBN 9781398413542 (Hardback)
ISBN 9781398463042 (ePub e-book)

www.austinmacauley.com

First Published (2021)
Austin Macauley Publishers Ltd
25 Canada Square
Canary Wharf
London
E14 5LQ

Chapter 1
Introduction

Why are you writing a book? That is a good question to ask any author. The answers would probably be as varied as the books. This book is written to challenge some widely held and deeply entrenched views about St John's Gospel. Many people, of course, would not dream of questioning its authority or reliability, but amongst those who study the New Testament as an academic discipline, there is a general approach that questions its relationship to the other Gospels and the historical Jesus and also its version of the original Christian message. This book is written to challenge that approach.

St John's Gospel itself very obligingly tells us why it was written. 'These are written so that you may come to believe that Jesus is the Christ, the Son of God, and that through believing, you may have life in his name' (20:31[1]). The fundamental purpose of the book is to increase faith.

Almost everything about the Gospel is questioned by someone, and even the sentence just quoted, which I believe

---

[1] Quotations are from the New English Bible except those indicated REB, the Revised English Bible.

is the basis for understanding the Gospel, is a matter of some uncertainty. One of the problems facing those who study any of the Gospels is that we do not have a first edition. The oldest versions we have are clearly copies of earlier manuscripts, and sometimes they are a little different. The explanation of why John wrote the Gospel, quoted above, occurs in different manuscripts with the Greek word for 'believing' in two different tenses of the verb, so that it could mean, as above, 'come to believe' or it could mean 'continue to believe.' The different interpretations have implications. Is this a book for people who do not know Jesus or for people who have committed themselves to him? Nonetheless, the motive is that of growing faith. John is emphatic that this is the means of gaining life, a rich and eternal life.

If it is fairly clear that the book has been written to develop faith, many would question how the author has pursued this aim. Has the author changed the details to fit a particular perspective on the Christian faith? Furthermore, is the understanding of Jesus and his significance something that has evolved some considerable time after the Gospel was first proclaimed?

The purpose of this book is to suggest that it is plausible to consider that the Gospel is as old as any writing in the New Testament, has a source that is very close to the original historical events and gives as profound and valid an explanation of the Christian message as can be had. I am going to suggest that the reasons usually given for thinking that the Gospel is a later work and perhaps distant from the original Christian message should be considered to be quite the opposite; reasons for thinking that the book represents a very early presentation of the life, death and resurrection of Jesus and the earliest of attempts to preach the good news.

I think the simple statement of the reason the Gospel was written is central to understanding the nature of the book and how we should view it in relation to the other books of the New Testament. My theme is that the Gospel is written out of a passionate desire to give as many people as possible the opportunity to share in the exuberant, transforming and limitless quality of life that having in faith in Jesus, the Christ, can bring.

Those who approach the Gospel from the world of academic theology are not, of course, dismissing the book. They treasure and value its insight into Christian message and the nature and purpose of Jesus Christ. The questions arise from its relationship to Matthew, Mark and Luke and how closely it portrays the teaching of Jesus.

I remember once being party to a conversation between a young enthusiastic student from an 'evangelical' theological training college and Professor C F D Moule, who was a Professor of Divinity at Cambridge University at the time. I cannot remember what the discussion was about, but when the student made some point quoting from the Gospel, Professor Moule said, "Ah, but that's in John's Gospel." The student was puzzled by this response. I realised that it reflected the generally held view amongst theologians that John's Gospel had to be seen in a different way to the other Gospels and much of the New Testament. Its authority was something apart.

This book seeks to question that approach; that John's Gospel is to some extent unreliable or secondary to Mark, which is with Matthew and Luke, the synoptic tradition. I shall try to do this largely by looking at the Gospel itself. Unless there is some totally unexpected dramatic discovery of new manuscripts, there can be no proof, but I believe there are good reasons for challenging the long-held and deeply entrenched views of the inferior status of John's Gospel.

Chapter 2
What's the Problem?

There is enormous variation in opinions and approaches to the Gospel from one extreme to the other. At one extreme are those who come from a background which approaches scripture without question or criticism and would not suspect a single sentence to be of doubtful historical truth or the very words of Jesus. For them, the book simply contains some of the most beautiful and precious words of Jesus. At the other end of the spectrum are some of those who coming from the world of Biblical criticism and academia have challenged almost every aspect of it. At times, it has been suggested as being written much later with no regard for historical facts, putting forward a changed theology, and even the writings of a separate sect.

Whilst most of the more extremely sceptical views about the book have not persisted, nonetheless the mainstream of non-conservative Biblical study continues to hold a general view of John's Gospel which puts it in a different status with regard to the historical Jesus and the early teaching of the church compared to the other three New Testament Gospels.

When John's Gospel speaks of the many books that could have be written about all the things Jesus did (21:25), the author surely never conceived of the enormous number of books that would be written about his own Gospel. I am not going to attempt to review or consider all the various ideas and arguments that have emerged and developed over many years. What follows is an attempt to sketch out how most non-conservative theologians now view the book.

Conventional academic view

The Gospel was written after Matthew, Mark and Luke probably either at the beginning of the second century or at the very end of the first century. Mark was the first Gospel to be written of which we have any knowledge. Matthew and Luke have used Mark as a basis for their Gospels, and as such there is a similarity in content and approach for which they are designated the Synoptic Gospels. Matthew and Luke share a further common source usually referred to as Q from the German Quelle for source. John's Gospel was written when the synoptic material was widely available, and whilst it was used as a basis for some of the narrative, it was not felt necessary to repeat the details which by then were well known.

The author is unknown but not John, brother of James and son of Zebedee. There may be links with another disciple who is designated as, 'the disciple whom Jesus loved'. The identity of this person is unclear. The Gospel perhaps arose from within a church that grew up around such an individual.

The purpose of the Gospel is a subject of more disagreement. What is clear is that it addressed the nature of Jesus' relationship to God and, in particular, develops the idea of his divinity, his identity with God himself. This implies a later evolution of Christian thinking, and by portraying it as the teaching of Jesus himself, it has created statements by Jesus that were, in fact, never said.

There is evidence within the book of influences from the Hellenistic world, and possibly some Greek philosophy has influenced the writing. The concept of a Johannine community which found itself under threat from traditional Jewish people is another widely developed theme.

It is undoubtedly clear that the chronology of events in the Gospel is very different from that in the Synoptics, and this is seen as fitting into some scheme of theological argument. Many have felt that the Gospel shows signs of repeated revision in the ordering of the contents. A common idea is that the book is constructed around seven themes corresponding to particular actions, 'signs', performed by Jesus.

The conclusion of these range of sceptical views is that the Gospel should be seen primarily as a work of theology which promotes a particular understanding of the nature of Jesus and that furthermore, this may not be true to the original teaching of Jesus and the early church. As such, it should not be considered a reliable historical source and that the words ascribed to Jesus may owe more to the thinking of the author than actual statements of Jesus. It is thus that for some people in some ways, the Gospel stands in a subordinate position in relation to the other Gospels and the early Epistles.

This, I hope, represents a broad quick view of the attitude which I am challenging. Of course, each major work on the Gospel has developed its own particular emphasis and ideas about the Gospel. However, I suggest that the preceding paragraphs represent a recognisable impression of conventional thinking about John's Gospel.

My purpose in writing is to challenge these views and both the assumptions from which they are derived and the conclusions which follow from them. Some may say that I have set up a straw doll to knock down. That this is a poor representation of advanced theological thinking. It may be something of a caricature, but certainly the view that the Gospel is later than the other three and represents a development in Christian thinking rather than an early position seems to be a very widely held opinion. My suggestion is that the Gospel was written at a very early stage in Christian thinking, without reference to or dependence on the Synoptic Gospels. As such, it is perhaps more historically accurate than them and gives the potential of getting as close to the historical Jesus as can be achieved through the New Testament.

"The fourth Gospel"

Before going any further, I want to mention what does strike me as a peculiar affectation that is applied to John's Gospel. It is often referred to as 'the fourth Gospel'. It is not customary to refer to Mark as the second Gospel. We have no idea who really wrote Mark's Gospel other than the church tradition. There is certainly no suggestion within the text itself that gives any indication whatsoever.

The same is true of Matthew's Gospel. Luke's Gospel does refer to the process of writing and, of course, links to the Acts of the Apostles. There seems no doubt that those two books have the same authorship. The presumption that it is Luke, Paul's companion, relies largely on the curious jump in the narrative from third person to first person plural during

Acts (Acts 16:10). Again, church tradition tells us that Luke is the author.

By using the title, 'the fourth Gospel,' attention is drawn to the differences from the other Gospels, and it gives a sense of uncertainty and doubt about the authorship but that is no less certain than for any of the other Gospels. Indeed, there is an attempt to ascribe the authority for its content within it, by stating that it is the witness of the disciple whom Jesus loved. The Gospel itself does not give that person a name. I am going to argue that it is John, but irrespective of that point, there is no good reason for not using the centuries old title of the book, and for the most part, I shall do this without wishing to beg the question of who wrote it. Why should we use a different type of designation for this book? It seems to be a slightly underhand way of subliminally questioning its authority. I shall refer to it as John's Gospel and use other titles purely for literary variation.

By what authority?

What new evidence have I got to challenge the long-established theories supported by many extremely highly qualified and learned academics over many years? None whatsoever. However, I do not consider there to be much evidence for any theory about John's Gospel. I do not recognise the sort of evidence that I have been used to expecting when in the past I have been engaged in medical research. There is very little material outside the New Testament itself, and much of the arguments have centred around trying to explain and understand the book in relation to the other documents of the New Testament and our understanding of the early church that derives from them. It is a matter of trying to sketch in the missing pieces.

My approach is that the most obvious is likely to be correct. That common sense should be the overriding factor in assessing ideas. We should stand back and look at the overall picture. There is a danger in close study of being unable to see the wood for the trees. I believe that much of the thinking on John's Gospel has taken as its starting point the position that it was written after the other three New Testament Gospels as something beyond question, and so the theories seek to address why it is different and how it came into being.

It is, I suggest, a common phenomenon in all areas of academic work that familiarity is confused with certainty. What I mean is this: a theory is proposed and finds merit. It is widely discussed and becomes used more and more. The more people refer to it and use it, the more it becomes an accepted fact. What has not happened is that anything has arisen which enhances the strength of the evidence that originally supported the theory. This can certainly happen in scientific work, and I believe it is true of the thinking about John's Gospel. It is an 'established fact' now that John's Gospel was produced after the Synoptics and must be considered in the light of their dominant status.

John's Gospel is of significance to Christians as a work to develop and understand faith. That same faith should lead us to accept that those who received the Gospel and decided it was valuable, reliable, and ultimately those who incorporated into the canon of the New Testament, were guided by the Holy Spirit.

I also think that we should accept that there some things we are never going to explain or understand. There will be elements that seem strange and inconsistent. We should not expect every detail to fit in with some 'cunning plan'.

My thinking about John's Gospel has developed over many years, but I was greatly influenced by the writing of John A T Robinson, known to my generation as the Bishop of Woolwich. He became famous appearing as a witness in the trial of the publication of *Lady Chatterley's Lover* and from a book *Honest to God* in which he outlined contemporary radical theological thinking for the lay audience. On him fell the anger of those who opposed such an approach. He had radical ideas on the dating of books in the New Testament, and when I first became aware of his ideas on John's Gospel, they fascinated me. I did not realise then that he had not published a detailed account of this. His detailed analysis and thoughts were eventually presented in a series of lectures. He started a book based on this but died before it could be finished and the work was published posthumously. I read it with great interest and it influenced my thinking.

The Priority of John[1] is a scholarly work and makes some remarkable claims. He even proposes a precise date for the crucifixion. His ideas have not been widely accepted, and I cannot follow all his arguments. I do think he made some very important and valid points. A central claim is that John's Gospel was produced very early on. He concludes that the latest additions were added before AD 65[2], and that the main body of the Gospel was written before this. This is, of course, a date as early as, if not earlier than, any suggested for Mark's Gospel which has generally been considered to be the first Gospel written.

He wisely draws attention to the difference between the assumption that something is authentic unless proved otherwise and the opposite attitude which is to assume that it is inauthentic unless there is good reason to think otherwise. He compares the former approach, as advanced by J Jeremias, with on the other hand, the presumption that it is inauthentic and a creation of the Christian community, the view adopted by Bultmann. He says, 'Neither presumption is in itself more scientific than the other, though it is often silently presupposed that the presumption of inauthenticity is more 'critical', thus implying an identification of criticism with scepticism: an equation common in the popular mind. Yet there can be uncritical scepticism as much as uncritical conservatism.'[3]

I shall refer to some of his ideas in what follows, but this is not simply an attempt to reproduce his thinking about John's Gospel. I think there are important points to be made about why the Gospel was written and how that motivation led to the style of the Gospel.

Dating the Gospel

A great deal has been written and discussed about the dates of the Gospels, when they were written. John's Gospel has been traditionally assigned a later date than the other Gospels. We need to ask what does the date of a Gospel mean? All our contemporary books have a date of publication, usually conveniently printed at the beginning. Publication is a commercial enterprise that has been going on a long time but it clearly is closely associated with printing. Once books were printed then multiple copies were produced in a relatively short space of time. Whilst books had to be handwritten, the very process of producing a book becomes a less clearly defined process. No doubt some authors at the time of Christ did employ multiple scribes to copy out lots of editions of their book for sale. It seems unlikely that the Gospels were produced in that way. In what way were the editions of the Gospels created?

We have a very limited knowledge about this. Were multiple copies made close to the time the book was first written or was that something that happened at a later time? Perhaps copies were made to order as individuals and, more likely, individual churches requested them. Whatever the sequence of events, it is clearly very different from the concept of publishing a book today.

The situation is further complicated by the concept of an oral tradition. Not only would stories and sayings have been circulated simply by word of mouth, but even books would be learnt by heart. Without literacy, books would be recited to groups or individuals and memorising them would be a far more normal process than would seem to us now. The tradition of learning the Koran is still very much alive in the Moslem world. Is it not very likely that one common and relatively cheap way of obtaining a copy of a Gospel was to get someone to learn it by heart?

These questions provide a basis for further consideration on the issues of when the text of a Gospel became fixed and how there might be different versions. The question that is fundamental to the concept of the 'date of the Gospel' is when the writing was created and its relationship to the development of the Christian Church and its understanding, and also most importantly, its relationship to the other Gospels. When people have maintained that John's Gospel is 'late', what they are generally saying is that it was written with the knowledge of the Synoptic Gospels. Opinions have varied on the extent to which the synoptic tradition was used or influenced the book. The other major concept is that it seeks to develop thinking beyond the stage that had emerged as a consequence of the Synoptics and many of the epistles.

I think that John Robinson's view that John's Gospel was written at a very early stage in the development of Christian thinking and that it was written without sight or influence of the other Gospels is correct. John Robinson's book is called *The Priority of John*, and that is entirely appropriate. The crucial issue is whether the Gospel is itself an original source and not dependent or secondary to the other Gospels. So I think that John's Gospel is not dependent on any other of the New Testament for its source of material but has its own direct witnesses. In addition, I also think that what it says beyond the factual accounts, that is its attempt to explore the significance of Jesus, is an early piece of Christian theology. That is a much more controversial idea and runs counter to most accepted views.

We cannot consider the date of a Gospel to be publication. The way these ancient books were distributed was so different from anything we now associate with that word. The question is more appropriately, when were they written? In isolation, this question has little significance. What matters is at what stage in the development of Christian thinking they were created and what was available as sources for the content. What oral sources and what written material could the writer draw upon? It is quite clear that Mark, Matthew and Luke share a great deal in common, and so are called synoptic.

Differences from the Synoptics

John's Gospel is markedly different from the Synoptic Gospels, Matthew, Mark and Luke, and those of the so-called Apocryphal Gospels, books not included in the canon of the New Testament, which have a credible claim to some attention. From the earliest days it was recognised that John's Gospel was different. Clement referred to it as a 'spiritual Gospel'.[4] The differences are emphasised by the fact that the other three Gospels are so very similar in many ways and contain very similar and at times identical wording.

The Synoptic Gospels share a great deal in content and the way in which they describe Jesus speaking, both the manner of speech and the sort of things he says. Many of the miracles described in Matthew, Mark and Luke are missing from John. The relatively few miracles that are described in John are mostly not found in the Synoptics. Thus in John, Jesus turns water into wine and raises Lazarus from the dead. The healing of the man born blind and the paralysed man by the pool of Bethesda do not correlate with any specific episode in Mark, Matthew or Luke. On the other hand, the feeding of the five thousand is in all the Gospels, and Jesus walking on water is in Mark and Matthew.

There are effectively no parables in John, and these are a major feature of the Synoptic Gospels. There are two passages about sheep and shepherds found in Chapter 6 which could be construed as parables and they will be discussed later, but if these are parables then they are the exception in this Gospel.

In contrast, the Synoptic Gospels draw attention to the use of parables by Jesus and give a wide range of examples.

John's Gospel contains no accounts of the appearance of angels. There are clearly instances in Matthew and Luke. Mark's Gospel has very little. We are told that angels waited on Jesus after the temptations in the desert, but the person who gives the message of the resurrection, often perceived as an angel, is actually described as a young man.

Then there is a distinctly different version of the timeline of the ministry of Jesus. In John, the events clearly occur over several, probably three years, and Jesus visits Jerusalem several times. In the Synoptics, only one visit to Jerusalem is described, the final climax, and there is no clear idea of just how long Jesus' earthly ministry was. In John's Gospel, Jesus clears the temple of traders near the beginning of his ministry, whereas in the Synoptics, it is part of the final few days. A very striking difference is that although John describes a Last Supper before Jesus' arrest, it does not include the institution of communion. Furthermore, the relationship of the crucifixion to the Passover is different. In John's Gospel, it appears to be the Sabbath, the day after the crucifixion, whereas in the Synoptics it seems to be the Friday. That is assuming that the festival was, as the Sabbath, from sunset on the day before and ending at sunset on the day. Thus in the Synoptics, the Last Supper on Thursday evening is the Passover meal.

Perhaps above all else is the way Jesus speaks and the sort of things Jesus says in John's Gospel. In the Synoptic Gospels, he tends to make short pithy remarks. In John's Gospel, he often speaks in quite lengthy passages. What he is talking about is different as well. He speaks about himself and in terms that are not found in the other Gospels. For example, he says to the disciples, "I came from the Father and have come into the world. Now I am leaving the world again and going to the Father" (John 16:28). It is in this Gospel that the famous, 'I am' sayings are found, nowhere else.

A superficial view of these differences might suggest that John is outnumbered, and the fact that there are three Gospels with a similar chronology and description indicates that John has probably got it wrong. However, the Synoptic Gospels are not three independent books describing the same events and words, each in their own way. They are at times word for word the same. There is no way that one of these books would get through a computer program looking for plagiarism. There is a synoptic tradition. Admittedly, there is the shared additional material which is not in all three Gospels and some that is unique to each but it seems to represent a common pool of memories and teaching.

A Book of Signs?

Those who consider John's Gospel to be historically inaccurate and a later development require an alternative explanation for its structure and content. This is generally on the basis of the symbolic nature of various events. The structure is usually considered to be based around a series of themes and is often referred to as 'The Book of Signs'.

The possibility of allegory and symbolism attract a great deal of study and theorising There are those who see symbolism everywhere in John. They will therefore find some representation for every detail in the Gospel, sometimes fairly cryptic explanations. It becomes very difficult to prove that these theories are untrue. I think this becomes something like the problem of conspiracy theorists. Once people become convinced that some event, say the assassination of John Kennedy, is the result of a conspiracy then it becomes impossible to dissuade them. Any evidence that seems to refute their theory is seen as part of the conspiracy. The crucial and truly scientific question that any conspiracy theorist should answer is, "What evidence would convince you that your theory is wrong?" This is, after all, the question every scientist must ask when attempting to prove a theory. The conspiracy theorist will probably not be prepared to contemplate any such approach. In the same way, those who are convinced that John's discrepancies are symbolic and evidence of the removed nature of his account, are unlikely to accept any argument to the contrary. However, the onus ought to be on them to prove that a sentence, a detail, a story, is not what it superficially appears to be but rather a representation of something else.

John's Gospel often gives explanations of details. There are no cryptic remarks such as, 'Let the reader understand' (Mark 13:14). The Gospel reads as an honest account of what was said and what happened. Why should we think otherwise?

Whilst the more extreme attempts at making the Gospel a series of encoded images of a special agenda are not followed by most theologians, there is a long tradition of describing the Gospel as 'The Book of Signs'.

This fairly standard view of the Gospel would see it split into seven major sections following an introductory section. John underlines the turning of water into wine at the wedding in Cana as the first sign, and so the theory views this as leading on to the theme of bringing in the new. The second sign is the official's boy who is healed. This has to be the second sign because the Gospel says it is.

After starting to enumerate signs, the Gospel ceases to do so. Whereas there are a whole number of incidents and discussions after the first sign, the Gospel moves on to the healing at the pool of Bethesda which is usually considered as the third sign.

The fourth sign is usually taken as the feeding of the five thousand with following statements about the bread of life.

The fifth sign is the man born blind and the subsequent statements about seeing and insight.

The sixth sign is the raising of Lazarus, and then the seventh sign is the crucifixion and resurrection.

This theory creates a picture of the Gospel as one which takes a series of major ideas about Jesus. Each section starts with a miracle, a sign, that Jesus performs which is an allegory of the theme, and then there are other incidents, sayings and dialogue which expand on the idea.

However, if one steps back and looks critically at the plan, it simply does not work. There are all sorts of episodes and points made which do not fit into this pattern, and the significance of others has to be stretched to fit the pattern.

The first sign is turning water into wine, but this is followed by a detailed account of Jesus clearing the temple that ends with Jesus referring to the resurrection in an enigmatic fashion by rebuilding the temple. There is no obvious link to water becoming wine and certainly no assistance is given in trying to show one. The next passage is the conversation with Nicodemus which speaks of the role of the Spirit and then the main message of the Gospel, the need to have faith in Jesus to gain eternal life. What follows is a dialogue about Jesus being the Messiah. There are several themes discussed here including baptism. Next is the long and detailed story of the encounter with the woman at the well in Samaria and the notion of living water, which certainly seems far removed from turning water into wine.

Only after all this do we have the second sign, the healing of the officer's son in Capernaum. In contrast to the 'first sign' there is no accompanying material for we move straight on to the healing of the man at Bethesda. What follows is Jesus declaring his close relationship to God as Son and the conflict with the Jews about this.

At the start of Chapter 6, what is in effect halfway through the book preceding the final discourses, trial, crucifixion and resurrection, we find the feeding of the five thousand. This is followed by a discourse on Jesus being the bread of life. At last there does seem to be a structure which fits with the concept of 'The Book of Signs'. Yet even here there is an interruption for the walking on the water which does not appear to have any relevance to the theme of bread and life.

There is a lot more narrative and detail before we reach the healing of the man born blind. Again this is followed by some discussion on spiritual blindness, but Jesus has already said, "I am the light of the world" (John 8:1) some way before the account of the healing. The raising of Lazarus includes within it the statements about Jesus being the resurrection and the life but there is no further material outside the story itself.

In conclusion, I do not think this model works at all. It is a view of the structure of the Gospel which does not correspond with common sense. If we start with the view that it is perfectly possible that the Gospel has a fairly accurate account of the timing of the events, then this forms the basis of the structure. What is clearly true is that at times the Gospel moves on from a description of an event to a quotation of Jesus or a description of him which relates to what has just been described. Thus after the story of the man born blind being given sight in Chapter 9, we have the statement of Jesus, "It is for judgement that I have come into this world—to give sight to the sightless and to make blind those who see" (John 9:39). It is surely entirely plausible that this statement is not related in time to the episode just described but could be easily associated with it as the story is recounted verbally. A more obvious example still is the collection of thoughts about Jesus as the bread of life which follow from the feeding of the five thousand. What of this is an account of what Jesus said at the time, things Jesus said on another occasion and perhaps things that the original source said when talking or preaching about it? I shall suggest that this is the Apostle John and that the Gospel structure reflects its major source of the preaching of John.

Instead of viewing the Gospel as a book constructed around a series of themes with total disregard to the sequence of events, we should consider it as formed from the words of the teaching and preaching of someone very close to Jesus, the Apostle John. Furthermore, the person writing, like us, is not entirely clear as to what are direct quotes of Jesus at the time, something Jesus said on another occasion or the interpretation of John.

References

1. Robinson, John A T (1985) *The Priority of John,* London: SCM Press.
2. Ibid p71
3. Ibid p3
4. Hill, C E (2010) *Who Chose the Gospels?* Oxford: Oxford University Press, p74.

Chapter 3
What is the purpose of the Gospels?

How did the Gospels come to be written?

Underlying the questions of when the Gospels were written, why there are several and their relationship to one another, is the basic problem of, how did the Gospels come to be written? It is fascinating to speculate on just how we move from an utterance of Jesus, or an observed event, to the words in the text, but it remains a mystery. It remains a major problem for understanding the relationship between the Gospels and the way they came to be written that we have no text before the second century. There is a void in our knowledge of how the Gospel content got from the events of about AD 30 to the second century, from when there are some surviving parts of the written Gospels.

If we consider what we know about the development of the church and the writings of the New Testament in the remainder of the first century from the end of Jesus' earthly life, then there is very little indeed apart from the books of the New Testament. We lack any truly independent historical evidence. There are a handful of brief mentions in the writing of the Jewish historian Josephus, some references in the rabbinic tradition, and a couple of early second century Roman historians, Tacitus and Suetonius, refer to the subject. These are not particularly useful historical sources. All they tell us is that they had heard of Jesus and the Christians. What they report is common gossip gained with no effort at accuracy or research.

Most of what we know of the early years of the church comes from the material that is in the New Testament and then references through early Christian writing. We have to accept that we do not know just how the Gospels came to be written nor where their material came from.

Those who heard Jesus speak, those who met him, and people who saw what he did would have vivid memories of these events. If they became part of the new church, then their experiences would be something they wanted to contribute and would be valued by the communities of which they were part. Thus inevitably there was some common pool of remembered material in circulation. However, to what extent was a Gospel constructed from this evolved communal knowledge and to what extent did it rely on the contribution of one or two eyewitnesses in the way that the classic story circulated by the early church fathers describes? Eusebius describes a book by Clement, who, in turn, is apparently repeating a tradition passed on to him by earlier elders of the church. This said that the Gospels which contain the genealogies of Jesus, that is Matthew and Luke, were the first of the four to be written, that Mark was written for those in Rome who had heard the Apostle Peter's preaching and wanted a record of it, and that John, 'last of all, composed a spiritual Gospel'[1].

This ancient tradition is essentially the reason that the Gospels are in the order that we find them in the New Testament. However, it gives no explanation at all of why three of the Gospels contain not only a very significant amount of the same material but also in places extremely close wording. Nearly all of Mark's Gospel is found in either Matthew or Luke and much of it in both. Furthermore, when the language is similar but not identical, the differences are usually because Matthew or Luke has added to Mark's wording. This all fits in with the theory that Mark was the first Gospel to be written and that Matthew and Luke used it as a starting point for theirs.

There is a less well-defined tradition in the church that Matthew's Gospel was written by the one of the twelve disciples who was a tax collector, that Mark was written with the direct guidance of St Peter, that Luke's Gospel was written by Paul's companion who had spoken to the Apostles and to Mary, the mother of Jesus, and that John's Gospel was written by another of the twelve, the brother of James. If these ideas were true, then the Gospels would be essentially the accounts of individuals who had been directly involved in what was described. These Gospels would be totally independent and distinct to each personality.

The close similarity in text of the Synoptics makes this a highly unlikely scenario. We simply do not know how the testimony of events involving a large number of people came to be collected into a single account and to what extent, if any, one of the central figures of Jesus' ministry had any input. The generally accepted view is that Mark's Gospel is the oldest of the three Synoptic Gospels and the basis for the other two.

However, I think we should seriously question the image of the Gospel writer sat at a desk, parchment in front of him and stylus in hand with a copy of Mark's Gospel to one side. The Gospels were probably written in different places and emerged from communities quite separate from each other. It is surely quite possible that the very lack of a written Gospel was the driving motive that caused the writer to produce the new Gospel. It is possible that there was someone there who knew Mark's Gospel by heart, but if, in fact, there was an oral tradition as the basis, rather than a written Gospel, then there is nothing illogical in supposing that all three Synoptic Gospels have a similar origin. The oral tradition is largely common but there are obvious differences. At some point and for reasons that we do not precisely know, there is a decision to turn the oral tradition into a written document, and each writer produces their own version. Such a scenario does not require that any writer had sight of any other written version and the precise temporal relation is quite irrelevant. That Mark's version should be shorter may reflect a more critical attitude to the material in the oral tradition and the writing style simply the consequence of the personality and education of the writer. It is not necessary to conclude that Matthew and Luke are branches from Mark as a common stem.

If a new church community had neither a written account nor someone who knew it by heart, then it would be natural to request a version of 'the tradition' about Jesus from another church community. This could be either in the form of an individual who had it learnt by heart or a written copy. If written copies were used in this way, it complicates our understanding of where Gospels first appeared. The association of a Gospel with a particular city might be the place to where it was first sent but written somewhere completely different.

In conclusion, there is a fog of uncertainty about how the memories, the witness accounts, and the remembered sayings of Jesus came to be written in the books we call Gospels. I suggest this uncertainty applies equally to all of the Gospels and not in any particular way to John.

By word of mouth

There is, it seems to me, a growing awareness of the role of memory in the early transition of the Gospels. James Dunn[2] relies heavily on the concept of oral tradition in his analysis. His concept is that there is an identifiable social phenomenon of communities remembering stories and events with key facts and things said in precisely the same words. Some details may vary, but there is a common core of salient facts.

Of course, the start of the Gospel tradition must have been remembered accounts. No one is suggesting that someone was walking around with parchment and stylus copying down what Jesus said and did. There are some descriptions which sound to be very direct memories. For example, the way that Mark records the words Jesus spoke to Jairus' daughter, "Talitha cum" (Mark 5:40). That sounds like a descriptive detail from the incident as recounted.

On the other hand, it seems inevitable that some of the Gospels as we now have them are words put in by the writers to construct a narrative. In St Mark's Gospel, for example, 'With many such parables he would give them his message, so far as they were able to receive it. He never spoke to them except in parables; but privately to his disciples he explained everything' (Mark 4:33–34) would seem to be more of a commentary rather than someone's remembered testimony.

If one accepted the tradition of Peter being the source behind the Gospel, then it could conceivably be his testimony, but even so what we have is an overall reflection and summary of what happened rather than a diary or everything he could remember.

Expressions like, 'On another occasion…' seem to be editorial rather than something handed down. At some point, the Gospels move from a series of individual memories from people or communities who had been witnesses to a structured text with a narrative structure. That is to say there is a story with a beginning, sequenced events, a climax and a conclusion. The question is, at what stage has that happened and to what extent? Most scholars would consider the Sermon on the Mount to be a collection of sayings by Jesus put together by an editor rather than the recollections of one particular teaching session.

An important point about the remembered tradition is to appreciate how normal and well-developed memorised stories and accounts were. Increasingly, we have become reliant on a variety of devices to retain information. The ease with which we can obtain writing materials and the widespread ability to read and write have meant that for a long time we have been used to the concept that we write down things we consider important and may wish to consult again. Now with calculators, computers and phones, even multiplication tables and some routine data that would have been commonplace knowledge half a century ago are becoming forgotten. In so doing, we tend to underestimate how good people can be at remembering things.

Today, only actors are expected to learn by heart long passages of text. They become good at it but it is not a particularly unusual or special ability. Young people can easily remember quite long passages of text without much difficulty. Those who make a point of it can learn a great deal. In the Moslem tradition, it is considered particularly worthy to learn the Koran and many people do. It is crucial to them that they are word-perfect.

If we now consider the world of first century Palestine and appreciate how difficult it would be to obtain writing materials and that few people could read and write, then we can see that learning a long passage of material about Jesus would be a normal and not particularly difficult task. Writing was a skilled task with the implements then available, and it was a profession to do it; such people were scribes. Paul did not write most of his own letters, and when he did add a few words at the end, they were not well written. He comments on their poor quality (Galatians 6:11).

This means that we should respect the remembered tradition of the Gospel material more highly than our current attitude to remembered material. There is, however, a further point. This is that surely even when the Gospels were put down in writing, it would still be very common and desirable to learn them by heart. One can imagine a church community who wanted a copy of the Gospel. It could well be that no one there could read, but even if there were some who were literate, the cost and problems associated with having a written copy would make it seem an extravagant and unnecessarily complex process. The obvious solution would be to get someone to learn it, word-perfect.

My suggestion is that this then leaves the Gospel in a form in which changes can be made, not lightly or carelessly but in a way that cannot be made to a printed book in our society. Take for example the opening verse of Mark's Gospel, 'The beginning of the good news of Jesus Christ, the Son of God' (Mark 1:1). Most modern versions now draw attention to the detail that the phrase 'the Son of God' is not to be found in the oldest manuscripts. The implication is therefore that it was not part of the original wording of the Gospel but has been added later. I suggest this is an example of the way the text might be altered. To make the point, consider the following fictional story.

It was Sunday evening in the small town of Dimitrya in what we now call Syria. In the house of Epaphras, preparations were underway for the meeting, the meeting on the Lord's day. Once people had finished their day's work, they would find their way from different parts of the town to this house through the narrow streets, bringing some food to share at the meal.

They were a varied collection of people, some quite wealthy with successful businesses buying and selling, others were slaves in service. There were men and women, young and old, but all were devoted to the new way, to follow Jesus the Christ.

They share together in breaking bread and remembering the Lord's death. Then they sit themselves comfortably on the floor and turn their eyes on young Demetrius. He has been sent away to Damascus to the bigger church there. He had been sent specifically to learn the Gospel. Demetrius had an agile mind and good keen memory. He had spent some time in Damascus hearing the Gospel and learning it by heart. The elders there had been very careful to make sure he had it word-perfect before they allowed him to return.

Everyone in the room had heard the Gospel several times now. They knew it well. They rejoiced in hearing the stories and the unfolding tale of the growing realisation by people as the account unfolds that this Jesus from Nazareth was the Christ, the Son of God. What they knew in their hearts to be the great saving truth is revealed step by step to disciples, followers, Jews and even Gentiles. The demons shout it out, Peter comes to an understanding, and the centurion at the crucifixion grasps the truth. So Demetrius stands, clears his throat, and conscious that all eyes are on him begins a little nervously, "Here begins the Gospel of Jesus Christ." The congregation bursting with the faith that has changed their lives respond with a loud voice, "The Son of God."

And so each time the Gospel is proclaimed, they insert those words, and it becomes part of the Gospel as they know it. It is for them the truth, and who is to say that this is not the work of the Holy Spirit. The Gospel may be God inspired in its words but perhaps not always in the sense of guiding the stylus on the parchment.

"Tell me the stories of Jesus" or tell me about Jesus?

So what do we have in the Synoptic Gospels? Are they, or at least is Mark, a collection of treasured anecdotes and remembered sayings cemented together by someone and committed to parchment? Is it the testimony of someone passed on and finally written down? Matthew and Luke clearly have beginnings which emphasise the presence of an author. The genealogy that starts Matthew is unlikely to be a piece of tradition handed down from eyewitnesses to Jesus' ministry. Luke gives us a statement that he is writing an orderly account but referring to the eyewitness accounts. There is more to the Gospels than simply all the things that people could remember about Jesus put together into a timeline. All the Gospels have the intention of leading to a deeper understanding of Jesus and the Gospel message. There are themes and aspects of his ministry that are emphasised. The writers have edited their material with a theological purpose. However, on the other hand, the supposition is that the writers did not simply sit down and write a book in which they invented Jesus saying and doing the sort of things which their understanding of the Christian faith gave them to believe he would have done.

But this is precisely what some people would claim the writer of John's Gospel did. They suggest that he created sayings to put into Jesus' mouth, the understanding of Christian theology which he wanted to convey. He perhaps used some recalled events but described them in ways which also fitted his purpose. That is the standpoint of an accepted critical approach to the Gospel. If on the other hand, we start with the notion that John's Gospel derives pretty directly from the witness of John, the disciple who was accompanying Jesus in his ministry, then the possibility arises that it is an accurate portrayal of Jesus' ministry and words, and the question would then be why the Synoptic tradition is different?

We keep returning to two crucial questions about the Gospels; why and when did they create them? I have already alluded to the point that a date of publication is a rather vague and not very useful concept. What is much more significant is the question of at what stage in the development of the church and of Christian theology were these books written. What prompted them to start writing?

We do not presume that the Apostles' immediate response to Pentecost was to call for papyrus and stylus to put down their memories of Jesus or dictate Christian doctrine. When did circumstances alter so that some people felt it necessary to write things down, and what was that change? Indeed, what were their objectives in writing? The books are clearly not simply biographies. When Mark commenced his book by saying that it was the 'Gospel' of Jesus, did he expect his readers to understand anything other than 'good news'? The book did not fit into a previously known genre. I have already said that we have no definite information on these points. We can make some suggestions and see how they fit into an overall pattern of our understanding.

Jesus is the Christ

The account in the Acts of the Apostles of the very earliest teaching after Pentecost is about the status of Jesus. The theme of Peter's sermons, Stephen's declaration, Peter's teaching to Cornelius is to affirm that Jesus is the anointed one, the expected one, the Messiah. The teaching is not to relay the words of Jesus. The message is not that Jesus has revealed God's nature to us and taught us that God is love and that all may come to him. It is not even that you are saved from the consequences of sin by what Jesus has done. Rather it is the simple message that Jesus is the Messiah which in Greek is Christ.

What is perhaps most surprising is that the Apostles assert that the evidence for this is that God raised him from the dead. The Gospels do not flinch from the fact that the resurrection is difficult to believe. They all recount doubt and that the revelation of the truth was often not immediate.

Mark describes how a young man tells the women at the tomb that he is risen. Their response is fear and that they tell no one (Mark 16:8). That appears to be the last words of the original version of the Gospel we have. What follows represents various possible additions. But these also say how the disciples did not believe the message (Mark 16:11,13). Luke's Gospel records how the women are told by men in dazzling garments of the resurrection, but when they report this to the disciples, 'the story appeared to them to be nonsense, and they would not believe them' (Luke 24:11). What follows then is the account of the two on the road to Emmaus who tell the unrecognised Jesus that the women have a story that Jesus is alive. After a long walk, it is only in the breaking of bread that they recognise him (Luke 24:31).

Matthew, at the very close of his book, tells of Jesus appearing to the disciples on a mountain in Galilee but includes the words, 'though some were doubtful' (Matthew 28:17). In John's Gospel, the doubt of Thomas is made an important part of the narrative. When Thomas is finally convinced, Jesus says, "Happy are they who find faith without seeing me." (John 20:29)

Thus this totally unprecedented event which is difficult to understand is given as the reason why people should accept that Jesus is the Christ. This is the starting point of the Gospel.

We do, of course, have one source only for the very earliest of the Christian teaching, namely the Acts of the

Apostles. We cannot view this as a completely objective historical source. Some of the later parts can be correlated with what Paul tells us about his life and ministry, although there do appear to be some discrepancies. However, there seems little doubt that the author is the same person that wrote Luke's Gospel as indeed it claims to be. Luke's Gospel contains a great deal of the teaching of Jesus and many details about his ministry, but that is not what he records the Apostles repeating in their preaching. When Peter addresses the crowd in Solomon's Portico of the temple, he tells them that Jesus is the person that the prophets have been predicting, "From Samuel onwards, every prophet who spoke predicted this time (Acts 3:24.") Preaching to Jews, Peter tells them that Jesus is the long-awaited Messiah.

John states that the purpose of the Gospel is to promote that same message. He has written so that people will come to believe that Jesus is the Christ, the Messiah. He goes on to say that this belief gives life. This is John's mission.

An important detail in the account of this early teaching is to note that they are not quoting sayings of Jesus. The Apostles and preachers did not see it as their task to transmit and retell the teaching that Jesus gave. The earliest message was not about what Jesus said, it was about Jesus himself. There is reference to the wonderful things he did but not as specific signs, just a supporting piece of evidence for the claim being made about him.

The first Christian message was not that Jesus was a wonderful person who said some really important things you must hear. Nor was it that Jesus has given us new insight into our relationship with God. It is the uncompromising assertion that Jesus was the expected one, the Messiah, and God has proved it by the resurrection. As Paul put it, "We preach Christ..." (1 Cor 1:23).

The very fact that the name that came to be applied to these followers of a new way was 'Christian' reflects that their teaching was about the Christ; that Jesus was the Christ.

What is also clear is that at a relatively early stage in church growth, the Christian Gospel was taken to and received by Greek-speaking people who did not see themselves as Jewish. The appointment of the deacons described in Chapter 6 of Acts makes this clear. The accounts of the ministry of Paul reveal a church rapidly spreading beyond the confines of Israel and reaching into the complex mixed cultures that surrounded it.

One can imagine their immediate response to this simple message would be that the Messiah was a Jewish concept. The Messiah was someone who was going to restore Israel to its ideal state. In the context of occupation, that would mean at least driving out the foreigners and bringing in a society based on a right relationship with God. These concepts would have had no relevance for them. The Apostles were at pains to say that the Messiahship of Jesus was not this but something quite different. That Jesus, the Christ, was a transforming power for all people everywhere; that being the Messiah was not about the restitution of an ideal Jewish state but a transformation of individuals' lives. The Apostles struggle to find the right language to express just what they mean, but they are clear that what is required fundamentally is a belief in Jesus himself rather than following his teaching.

I suggest that it is in this context that John comes to write his Gospel. It is an attempt to make clear to people who are not Jewish that Jesus is for them a transforming necessity. The repeated plea in John's Gospel is to believe in Jesus and that through this belief will come life.

Thus the Gospel is written to assert that Jesus was not just a messenger from God, nor someone selected by God to free the Jewish people and restore the nation to its former glory, but someone of supreme importance for everyone everywhere. Jesus had a unique relationship to God, and in John's Gospel, we find this expressed in a variety of ways and expressions.

It is in this context that I believe John was written: the crucial need to explain to people everywhere, particularly those who did not see themselves as Jewish, why faith in Jesus was all important. Consequently, John's Gospel is not so much about what Jesus did and said, when compared with the Synoptics, as who he was and how we can have faith in him. The stories and sayings in John are all with this one objective to reveal Jesus, his nature and our relationship to God through him.

I suggest that this imperative was at a very early stage in the development of the Christian church. John's Gospel is about the nature of Jesus and his importance for people because that was what the church was trying to understand and express in its earliest days. People have often thought that John's writing on Jesus represents a reflection on the nature of Christ that emerges as time passes and theology develops. However, I suggest that its subject is reason to think that it is an early piece of writing and thinking about Jesus. One of the main reasons that have led people to view John's Gospel as a later work is, in fact, a good reason to think exactly the opposite.

The need for history

A turning point or perhaps more appropriately one should say a period of profound change must have been when the church came to realise that the expected second coming was not happening anytime soon. It is clear from Paul's writing that the earliest Christians envisaged the complete overthrow of the existing world order with the coming of Christ in glory within a human generation.

As the eyewitnesses died off and time passed, one can imagine that people then became concerned to keep accurate records of what they knew about Jesus. As the church grew and more and more, people came to follow Jesus and see him as the route to life, then they would want to know all they could glean about what he said and did. The business of collating and preserving the Jesus story would become a high priority.

That is not to say that the writers were simply compiling memorabilia. They too wanted to help people know Jesus and understand his relationship to God, but it would be important to include all that could be remembered of what Jesus had said and done. As the church started to encounter more and more resistance and then persecution and people had to start making all of life's complex decisions in the light of their new faith, then Jesus' teaching and his examples became a powerful resource they were grateful to receive.

Expressing the divine nature

One of the issues that had to be explored was the way in which the emerging church saw Jesus as one with God; that he was divine. Clearly, they believed he was separate from

God. Jesus is seen as teaching about God, praying to God, seeking to do God's will. God is something other than Jesus. However, they also have some sense that the relationship was such that they shared something of a common nature; that Jesus' relationship with God was different from any other human.

In the world of the time, there were many concepts of divinity. Roman emperors became gods, and the complex tradition of Greek mythology, Roman practice and the influences from other parts of the world mean that just to say that Jesus is divine begs more questions than it answers. Christianity emerging from the profoundly monotheistic Judaism was not going to easily accept the divinity of Jesus, yet there was something important that the church felt it had to express. It struggled, and those who wrote laboured to put it into words. No clear explanation of this emerged. There was not then as there is not now. What we have is a variety of attempts to come to terms with what they believed to be the truth.

Matthew and Luke have stories of the Nativity which include ideas that make Jesus' parentage different from all others, the Virgin Birth. The Synoptics also include the Transfiguration which reveals Jesus as different.

The opening of John's Gospel is justly famous for its opening, and the very familiar preamble used for the King's College Christmas Eve carol service speaks of John 'unfolding the mystery of the incarnation.' The wording is more subtle and appropriate than might at first be thought. To say that the mystery is unfolded is not to say that it is resolved, explained or solved. The mystery is revealed, opened out to view and presented. The mystery remains. A quotation I heard but I cannot attribute is, 'A mystery is something about which the last word cannot be said.' That is a very apt description and applies to the incarnation. I believe John presents a mystery; that is something that he himself cannot fully explain or understand.

Those who study the New Testament often speak as though their task is to unravel and reveal what the writers of the various books meant and intended. From this standpoint, the things that need explaining or are different from our first impressions are because of our failure to understand the writer's intention. I suggest this is wrong. In this case in particular, it is the writers themselves who are not clear on just what they are saying, what they mean. John himself cannot really produce a consistent entirely comprehensible explanation of what we know as the incarnation, the divinity of Christ.

John explores the relationship with statements such as "The Father and I are one," and, "Anyone who has seen me has seen the Father." The Gospel begins with its powerful way of linking God and Jesus through, 'the Word.' I do not think there is an entirely consistent sense of just what the relationship between God and Jesus is. This is something that the writer was struggling with, probably struggling with in his own mind but certainly struggling to put into words.

Paul's message about Jesus

Whilst the view that John's Gospel is an early work is controversial, there is general agreement that the earliest writings in the New Testament are the letters of St Paul. His letters are to the gentile world; that is to say to Greek-speaking people who do not consider themselves as Jews.

I believe that Paul has the same fundamental issue running through his writings. He too is trying to explain the significance and importance of Jesus to people for whom the Messiah seems like an irrelevant Jewish concept.

Paul has a different perspective and uses different words to get the message across. For Paul, brought up as a Pharisee, the failure of Jewish law, the inevitability of human nature to do the wrong thing, to sin, require the transformation of Jesus. The problem is universal. The Jewish law fails to solve the problem. The solution is Jesus.

Paul's writings are on a mixture of subjects. Often, they address particular problems, arguments and issues within churches, but there is also a repeated statement of the Christian Gospel as he understands it. Paul speaks of being saved by Jesus. For him, the sacrificial nature of the cross is important. Through the cross, Jesus saves us from the consequence of sin; that is death. This is not a study of the teachings of St Paul, but as well as the at times quite mundane and detailed problems of life for early Christians that he writes about, there is the recurring theme of the Gospel, that is Jesus Christ, crucified and risen. "We preach Christ," says Paul.

Jesus Christ fills his letters, but what is absent is an account of Jesus' teaching. The fact is that they contain, apart from a couple of exceptions, no teaching of Jesus. The exceptions themselves emphasise the fact by the curious way in which they are presented by Paul.

Paul is writing before any written Gospel exists, so he cannot quote them. However, the oral tradition must have existed, and indeed Paul refers to a tradition about the Lord's supper (1 Cor 11:23) but curiously says it came to him from the Lord himself. Perhaps more clearly is the example of when talking about the resurrection, he speaks of the facts which had been imparted to him (1 Cor 15:3). This seems to acknowledge the existence of a body of details about Jesus that have been handed on. However, it forms such a minute part of his writings.

He frequently refers to scripture as he knows it, sometimes to what seem to be early hymns, but not to the words of Jesus himself. He argues his case by analogy, by tradition, by our understanding of the Gospel. Surely you would expect him to say, 'as our Lord said...' or 'when Jesus healed...' or some other incident in his life. He does refer regularly to the crucifixion and the resurrection which for Paul is the heart of the Gospel. Jesus is the Christ; he was crucified and rose again.

The lack of the sayings and teachings of Jesus is not a minor odd detail; it is a fundamental question about the way Paul was preaching the Gospel. For Paul, the Gospel is Jesus Christ, not his teaching. The Christian church began by proclaiming Jesus, Jesus the Christ and his crucifixion and resurrection. It did not start by relaying the teaching of Jesus.

Some people suggest that Christianity started out as a set of thoughts, good ideas and examples by a good man, Jesus, who was crucified and that subsequently, as the cult of his followers grew, the idea that he was resurrected and that he was divine was incorporated into the teaching. The picture that emerges from looking at the oldest accounts we have says exactly the opposite. The teaching began with the nature of Jesus, the belief in the resurrection and the need for people to have faith in the Christ before everything else.

The very few instances of Paul quoting Jesus are exceptional not only in the small number but in the way he uses them. The most famous and obvious is the one mentioned above, the institution of the Lord's supper in 1 Corinthians 11.23, "For the traditions which I handed on to you came to me from the Lord himself: that on the night of his arrest the Lord Jesus took bread..." Firstly, Paul is referring to a tradition and one that he has already taught. What does he mean that it came from the Lord himself, and to Paul? He is surely not suggesting that as part of his Damascus Road experience Jesus slipped in the details of Holy Communion. Indeed, what does it mean that it comes from the Lord when it is a description of something Jesus said and did?

The emphasis seems to be that this is something that can be relied upon as authentic. Paul is convinced that he has here a direct account of what Jesus said and the all-important instruction to do this as a memorial, in remembrance. It is intriguing that Paul sees an appropriate way of emphasising the authority of this saying is to state that it comes directly from Jesus. It underlines that fact that most of his teaching is not relaying things that Paul believed Jesus to have uttered.

The other equally intriguing example is from the same letter when talking about marriage. "To the married, I give this command, not I but the Lord, that the wife should not separate from her husband" (1 Cor 7:10). What fascinates me about this is the way Paul, almost casually, drops this in amidst various rulings of his own which he freely admits are his not the Lord's. There is, it seems to me, almost a lack of reverence for the words of Jesus. One cannot imagine a contemporary church leader giving instruction on Christian behaviour and tossing in a precise statement of Jesus as though it was of little more consequence. One would imagine a statement along the lines of: on this particular point we have a clear ruling that comes directly from the teaching of our Lord himself.

Perhaps one can also note the way that, twice in his letters, Paul refers to the Spirit and the Spirit of God's Son enabling us to cry, 'Abba, Father' (Rom 8:15; Gal 4:6). 'Abba' is an Aramaic word and is quoted by St Mark as the word used by Jesus in his passionate prayer in Gethsemane (Mark 14:36). It has long been suggested that this was a particularly familiar form of address to a father and a distinctive style that Jesus used and taught his disciples to use, becoming a common liturgical expression in the very early church. There is some uncertainty about this theory but Paul does not usually use Aramaic words ('Maranatha' being an exception), and it seems very likely that he is in some way quoting a tradition going back to Jesus. However, he does not say that or in any way suggest that this is the word Jesus used. The message itself is more important to Paul than quoting Jesus.

Paul has a resource of stories and sayings of Jesus but he does not think these are the crucial component for building up the faith and developing the new Christians. For Paul what is fundamental is that people understand the significance of Jesus Christ.

That, I believe, is the crucial message of John's Gospel, and that is why it has the structure and content that it does. The emphasis on the relationship of God to Jesus, the idea of Jesus as the Word, the focus on the nature of Jesus through the 'I am' sayings, are features of the primary purpose of the gospel at an early stage in the development of the church. Whereas for many people these features are reasons for thinking that John's Gospel is a later work, I believe that they are the very reason for thinking that it is quite the opposite. This is the first major issue for the new church. Jesus is the Christ, that is something of profound significance for all the world, and how should we explain that?

Relationship between Synoptics and John

I suggest that as Christian thinking and teaching developed, people started to consider how the message about the Christ was revealed in the remembered sayings, encounters and actions of Jesus. This sounds rather as though I am suggesting that the Synoptic Gospels are secondary to John. That is to overstate the position. What I think needs stressing is that it appears that at the earliest stage of spreading the Christian message, the emphasis was not on Jesus' parables, teaching and miracles but on the revelation of Jesus as the Christ and his intervention through the cross for humankind. John is part of that early motivation.

What then is the relationship between John and the Synoptics? There has been a difference in opinion in scholars as to whether John had sight of one or more of the Synoptic Gospels. I think it is highly unlikely. Partly this is because I think it is likely that it was written before Mark, Matthew and Luke were widely circulated. I think more significantly is that it contains so many details that are not in the Synoptics and frequently there are differences. If he was simply copying a story out of their tradition, why did he not get it right? Why would he omit the institution of the Lord's Supper and why change the timing of the Passover in relation to the crucifixion? John is different because it was written without the influence of the other three Gospels and before they were widely known.

My conclusion is that John's Gospel is quite independent of the Synoptics. I believe that its central theme of the nature of Christ, his relationship to God and the vital importance to every person of having faith in Jesus, represent the earliest of writings and concerns for the church. This is the beginning of Christian understanding, not a later reflection and development.

References

1) Hill, C E (2010) *Who Chose the Gospels*, Oxford: Oxford University Press, p74.
2) Dunn James D G (2011) *Jesus, Paul and the* Gospels, Grand Rapids Michigan: Eerdmans, Chapter 2.

Chapter 4
John's Gospel: The One with Problems?

Are the Synoptics less problematic?

Those with the approach to John's Gospel which seeks to suggest that it is less authentic are quick to point out problems with the Gospel, points that seem inconsistent or unlikely. However, the other three Gospels all have their own issues. Before looking in detail at the features in John's Gospel which lead people to question its status, I think it is appropriate to point out some of the issues that are difficult to understand or explain in the Synoptic Gospels.

There are apparently only 31 verses in Mark's Gospel that are not in either Luke or Matthew[1]. However, one-third of Mark is not found in both Luke and Matthew, so that most of that third (the total Gospel is 661 verses) is found in one or the other.

So what is going on here? This is a problem. It is not without solution, but there is little evidence to guide us to the correct answer. Are Matthew and Luke using Mark in some form as a reference on which to base their writing and then exercising a judgement on the basis of their particular theological agenda as to which part to omit? Clearly, they have additional material, and some of this is shared between them—the so-called Q material. On the other hand, it may be that all three Gospels have a common source of material and that although Mark's Gospel is often considered as the initial primitive Gospel so to speak, in fact, it may itself be a derivative, albeit with less modification and addition from this common prior source: proto-Mark.

Whatever the correct explanation, one has to wonder why the Gospel writers on the one hand stick very closely to the same words and yet on the other do not do so completely. Luke, unlike the other two Synoptic Gospels, starts his writing with some explanation of why he is writing and from where he has obtained his material. He refers to the existence of other accounts. Indeed, he speaks of 'many writers' and that the traditions are from 'the original eyewitnesses'. Luke claims to have gone over the events in detail but then proceeds to use a lot of the exact text found in Mark and Matthew.

Matthew and Mark make no attempt whatsoever to explain where their accounts come from. Is it not peculiar that Luke does not try and correct this? If one was attempting to improve on a previous account, would one not say so, explaining how you had obtained further, more accurate information? I suggest that the correlation and disparity between the three Synoptic Gospels is a curious matter.

Another well-recognised problem is the ending of Mark's Gospel. There is a general consensus that the verses beyond verse 8 of the last chapter are a later addition. The oldest manuscripts end at this point and the style and content suggest a different writer. There are differences in how much and just what is added in the manuscripts that contain more than the first 8 verses of chapter 16.

There are, therefore, good reasons for thinking that the 'purest' of the Synoptic Gospels has some added material. This, however, is the least of the problems that so arise. The ending of the Gospel at verse 8 is decidedly odd and has provoked a vigorous and longstanding debate. Indeed, it has been called 'the greatest of all literary mysteries' according to Nineham[2].

One possibility is that the ending has been lost for some reason. This could be a purely physical accident or it might be that it was struck out because of disagreements on its content.

It is also possible that the Gospel was incomplete; that for some reason Mark was intending to add more but was prevented. However, there are many who believe that this was the intended original ending. If so, there remain further problems.

One issue that I have no competence to comment on is on the Greek syntax. The final word is the conjunction 'for' (γαρ). Some scholars consider this to be an unacceptable ending of a sentence let alone a book, whereas others are happy that it may simply reflect a rather crude literary style.

More disturbing is the meaning of the final sentence. The women have just discovered an empty tomb and been told by a youth that Jesus is risen. They are instructed to announce the resurrection and to convey a message to the disciples and Peter that they are to go into Galilee where they will see him. The final sentence informs us that they disobeyed both instructions. It ends by saying that they were afraid.

This is neither an omission of the resurrection nor a clear and satisfactory proclamation of it. Whilst some may argue that this is a highly theologically significant message, it is far from clear to most people and it remains highly surprising if not actually unacceptable. If the writer is intending people to know that the body of Jesus was raised from the dead, then to end this great book with the announcement that the first people who learnt of it were disobedient and terrified is a ridiculous piece of composition.

Whilst the ending of Mark's Gospel is a well-recognised problem, there is, it seems to me, another major conflict much less often discussed. This is the problem of the birth narratives.

It is well known that only Matthew and Luke contain stories of Jesus' birth and that they are different. Our familiarity with these stories particularly through nativity scenes and plays distracts us from the fact that they contain very little in common and are surely incompatible.

They both agree that Jesus was born in Bethlehem, that Mary was his mother and Joseph the father. They both attest the 'Virgin Birth'; that is to say that they tell us that Jesus was conceived by the will of God through the Holy Spirit and not the normal method of reproductive activity. In so doing, they are trying to say something about the unique relationship between Christ and God. Quite what they understood to be the process is impossible for us to know as they had a very different understanding of procreation. They did not, for example, have to grapple with the question of just what Jesus' chromosome composition was and where did it come from.

Matthew's Gospel makes no mention of Nazareth until the very end of the story. Only when the Holy Family returns from Egypt do we hear about Nazareth, and the account suggests that they were directed to Galilee to avoid another hostile king of Judea and that Joseph settled in Nazareth as though he had no previous connection with it. In contrast, Luke tells us that Mary and Joseph were in Nazareth before she conceived, and Luke provides us with an explanation of why they were in Bethlehem when Jesus was born.

Despite the universal assumption that Jesus was born in a stable, Luke does not, of course, actually mention it. He speaks of Jesus being in a manger. It is a reasonable assumption that they were in the stable of the inn as he also tells us that there was no room in the inn. However, Matthew refers to the magi going into the house. Of course, it is perfectly reasonable to assume that Matthew is not suggesting that they arrived within the first 24 hours of the birth. If anything, the astronomic event would coincide with the birth, and there would then be the lengthy journey from 'the east'. In fact, the detail that Herod ordered the killing of children under the age of two 'corresponding with the time he had ascertained from the astrologers', indicates a long time period.

The family departs into Egypt then, but this sequence of events does not tally with that described by Luke. He says that after the time of purification, a matter of a few weeks, they went to Jerusalem where they encountered Simeon and Anna and then 'they returned to Nazareth'. This contradicts Matthew. These two extremely well-known accounts of the circumstances surrounding the birth of Jesus raise some major difficulties in reconciling them.

In an entirely different episode, Matthew's Gospel contains what seems to me a clear mistake. This is in the account of the entry into Jerusalem. The other three Gospels all describe this event and state that Jesus rode a donkey or colt into Jerusalem. Matthew has a most peculiar description. The disciples are sent to the village of Bethphage, and there they find two animals, a donkey and her foal. They are both untied and brought to Jesus and both were covered with their cloaks. Jesus somehow rides them. (Matthew 21:4). Of course, the passage goes on to explain that this is to fulfil a prophecy from Zechariah. Indeed, there in Zechariah 9:9 we find the verses with the imagery described in Matthew. What is surely meant here is a piece of poetry and that there is repetition within it, repetition that emphasises the point. The king comes in gentleness, not on a war horse, but on an ass; not just an ass but the young of an ass, not a very big animal at that.

Matthew's Gospel has taken this piece of poetry and literally converted it into a description of what has happened, giving Jesus the difficulty of coping with riding two animals. Of course, it is strictly possible that there were two animals and that one was used to provide relief for the other during the journey. But surely the words in Zechariah are poetry and the image is of only one animal. The fact that Matthew so closely follows the words makes me believe that his description is not historically accurate but more influenced by the prophecy than eyewitness accounts.

Another problem that we find in the Synoptic Gospels is the apparent contradiction between Luke and Matthew about what the disciples were told to do and where they went after the resurrection.

We have already noted the enigmatic ending to Mark's Gospel. It contains so little, but the message given to the women, which according to the Gospel they did not pass on, was that they would see Jesus in Galilee.

This message is repeated in Matthew, but in addition, there is the description of these women encountering the risen Jesus on their way to tell the disciples. This time the message is explicitly that the disciples are to go into Galilee. This is, of course, the implication of the first message in Mark and Matthew, but now it is clearly made to be an instruction.

Matthew goes on to say that the disciples followed Jesus' instruction and made their way to Galilee, and there Jesus appears to them on a mountain. This forms the conclusion of the Gospel.

On the other hand, in Luke's Gospel, in addition to the message from angels to the women at the tomb, Jesus appears to the two on the road to Emmaus, to Peter and then to the eleven and 'the rest of the company'. Furthermore, Jesus then instructs them to stay in Jerusalem, "I am sending upon you my Father's promised gift; so stay in this city until you are armed with the power from above" (Luke 24:49).

There seems to be a contradiction between these two accounts. Luke's account fits in with his subsequent description of Pentecost in Acts. John describes Jesus appearing to the disciples in Jerusalem. There is no instruction about going to Galilee, but then the final story is of an appearance on the shore of the Sea of Tiberias. John has already in 6:1 identified this as the Sea of Galilee.

One has to accept that this period is one of contradicting accounts. It seems to me pure prejudice to consider John's Gospel as in some way less reliable when there is clearly conflict in the synoptic accounts.

Although traditionally, theologians have picked on John's Gospel as the most distant from historical accuracy, there are reasons for considering Luke's Gospel as the most difficult to reconcile. We have just seen the problem with the post-resurrection events, and it has its own unique account of the nativity. In Luke, people apparently spontaneously burst into poetic utterance, so Zechariah at John's naming, Mary at the annunciation and Simeon at the presentation in the temple.

The long reflective passages in John and, in particular, the High Priestly Prayer are seen by many as evidence of the secondary nature of this Gospel. However, in the Synoptic Gospels, how do we have descriptions of events that would seem to be private to Jesus: the temptations, the Garden of Gethsemane?

The Synoptic Gospels contain accounts of Jesus' prayer and dialogue in situations which would appear to be totally private. There is the prayer in the Garden of Gethsemane. It is, I suppose, possible to argue that the waiting disciples manage to hear as much as is recorded before they fell asleep. If that is the case, it increases their misdemeanour as a callous disregard for the words of anguish being uttered by Jesus. It is surely more likely that the words are not meant to be those overheard by them.

Whatever view one takes of the Garden of Gethsemane, the words of Jesus' temptation in the desert are clearly not overheard. What then is meant to be the source of this dialogue? There are only three options: that Jesus told his disciples what had happened, they were given to the Gospel writers in some miraculous way or they are the creation of the Gospel writers to make a theological point. Whichever option you prefer, it is a major issue about the Gospels.

These are just some of the issues that one can consider about the Synoptic Gospels. This is not an attempt to discredit the Gospels or undermine their authority. There is a great deal more that could be said about each of these issues. The reason I have drawn attention to these points is to demonstrate that it is not a question of plain sailing with Matthew, Mark and Luke whilst John is problematic. All the Gospels raise puzzles and questions. John is no different in this aspect from the other three Gospels. There is plenty in all the Gospels for people to analyse, debate and stretch the mind.

References

1. Williams, C S C (1962), 'The Synoptic Problem' in Black M and Rowley H H (eds.) *Peake's Commentary on the Bible*, London: Nelson, p748.
2. Nineham, D E (1969) *St Mark*, Harmondsworth: Penguin Books, p439.

Chapter 5
What is the Source of the Gospel?

Identity of Beloved Disciple

If, as I am suggesting, the synoptic tradition is not John's source for the story of Jesus, then what is? The Gospel tells us that the authority is 'the disciple whom Jesus loved'. At the end of the Gospel is this strange statement which seems to invalidate itself, 'This is the disciple who is testifying to these things and has written them, and we know that his testimony is true' (John 21:24). There is a clear and sensible assertion that the beloved disciple is the source, it is his testimony that has been recorded in the Gospel. That he had written the Gospel is a possibility, but it is slightly peculiar to state all this in the third-person singular. However, the statement then goes on to speak in the first-person plural that the testimony is true. Who are the 'we'? It makes no sense for this part to be written by the beloved disciple. Then in the most teasingly enigmatic way, the final assertion is in the first-person singular.

Putting aside the clumsy assertions that form the last few sentences of the Gospel, it is clear that the Gospel is claiming that the disciple whom Jesus loved is the source of the material. The Gospel makes several references to this person. He is at the Last Supper next to Jesus, and at Peter's suggestion asks the identity of the one who is to betray him. He accompanies Jesus' Mother at the crucifixion and is commanded to look after her henceforth. He runs with Peter to the tomb at the first discovery of the empty tomb. His transformation of faith on entering the empty tomb is described. He is the subject of a conversation between Peter and Jesus at the post-resurrection meeting by the lake.

The question then is, who is this person? This is a matter of much debate. Many critical scholars have sought to argue that this is a different person to John, the son of Zebedee. However, I think the evidence supports the view that it is one and the same person, brother of James, and with Peter one of the apparently three most important disciples. Why would the Gospel hide its source behind the title if it was not thought well-known to whom it referred? I think the title, the disciple whom Jesus loved, is a particular title of respect given by the community around him to this person.

What are the reasons for thinking that the beloved disciple is the Apostle John? Firstly, there is, of course, a longstanding tradition going back to early Christian writers that the Gospel was written by the Apostle John. These early writers were not researching their material in the ways and to the standards required of academic study today. In fact, it may be that without realising it, they are quoting the same source which might or might not be accurate. It is easy to be critical of these traditions, but on the other hand, it is totally illogical to assume they are wrong simply because they are traditions. This evidence needs to be noted but is of limited value.

The most important and simple reason for believing that the author is the son of Zebedee is that if it is not John, then the Apostle is missing from the Gospel. The only John mentioned in this Gospel is the Baptist. The other Gospels make it clear that with Peter and James, John was one of the three disciples closest to Jesus and central to the events. Why should this Gospel leave this person out? Acts has Peter and John taking the lead right at the beginning of the church. It would be extremely bizarre if this significant person in the early Church is not mentioned. In fact, the Gospel of John is good at telling us when different disciples are involved in incidents. Although the Gospel never gives us a list of the twelve disciples, it is in this Gospel that we hear about Andrew, Philip, both Judas Iscariot and the other one, Thomas and Peter, of course, saying things or taking particular actions. Surely John is there too but with his special title.

When the Gospel does refer to John, it is clearly John the Baptist. In this Gospel, there is no need to put that qualification, the Baptist, because when the name John is used, it is used only for the Baptist. One cannot believe that whenever it was written, the author was oblivious of the status of Peter, James and John. It would surely be necessary to distinguish or make it clear which John was being mentioned. The implication is that the title of 'the beloved disciple' was known to be the Apostle John, brother of James and son of Zebedee.

There is another piece of evidence and that is the epilogue to the Gospel, Chapter 21. This passage raises a whole number of questions and so limits its weight in this argument. Nonetheless, even if this passage was written at a later date and by someone different from the rest of the Gospel, the person of the beloved disciple is part of the story, and whoever wrote it must have had their understanding of who that person was. Only if the distance between the rest of the Gospel and this passage is so great that a misconception has arisen, can the significance of the connection be disregarded. It is unlikely that there is a huge difference in time, for an important part of the story is the statement about this disciple potentially living to see Jesus return. The account emphasises that Jesus did not state that this would happen, only that it was not a matter of concern for Peter. There is surely a strong implication that the motivation for this passage is that the beloved disciple has died and that there was a widespread belief that Jesus had promised that he would live to see the second coming. People were therefore distressed about this. If this is the case, as seems likely, then it is unlikely that the author did not know the identity of this figure.

The description of the episode by the lake tells us who was there. In view of the controversy that has developed about the identity of the beloved disciple, I wish the author had been a little more explicit about who was in this group. Simon Peter, Thomas and Nathanael are named along with the sons of Zebedee. There are also two other disciples who are not named. As the narrative continues, it is quite clear that the beloved disciple is one of the party. If he is not John, the son of Zebedee, then he can only be one of 'two other disciples'. Given the extreme importance ascribed to this person throughout the Gospel and the significance for this whole story, then it would be a bizarre way to initially mention his presence. This leads to the conclusion that he has been named as one of the sons of Zebedee. A minor additional point is that this group were fishing and so it would seem that the beloved disciple was a fisherman which is, of course, what the sons of Zebedee were.

I find it difficult to understand why so many find it hard to accept the simplest conclusion that John the son of Zebedee and the disciple whom Jesus loved are one and the same. One cannot escape the suspicion that this is because it would mean that the source is indeed someone very close to Jesus and so challenges the long-held and widely accepted view that the Gospel is historically unreliable and removed to some extent from the teaching of Jesus.

I do not think it is difficult to imagine why the title came into use. If indeed John was the disciple with whom Jesus had a close friendship apart from that of Master and Disciple, then that is something which would place him in high esteem amongst the Christian Church.

It is quite plausible, particularly in view of the tradition that John was one of the longest surviving disciples, that he was a young man when he first followed Jesus. As such the relationship would have a different basis than with the older men, some of whom were married and who were more experienced in the ways of the world. When Jesus in his dying moments entrusts the care of his mother to him and asks his mother to care for him, it suggests a very close bond and one where it was recognised that he still needed parental support.

If John then builds around himself a church, it is easy to imagine that they would feel privileged to have as their leader the Apostle who had this close personal tie to the Lord. Would they not evolve this special title and as a measure of their respect always refer to him with these words? One thinks of the way Moslems speak of the prophet Mohammed. They often follow mention of him by the phrase, 'blessings and peace be upon his name.' Is it not quite likely that those who were in the community following John would add a phrase such as 'the disciple whom Jesus loved', after mentioning him and that in time, the name itself disappears and the phrase became the title used?

Who wrote the Gospel?

If my views are correct, then the Apostle John is the source of the Gospel and that his account of the events are not derived from another Gospel tradition. His Gospel message is an early attempt to help those first learning about the Christian message to understand the central truth of the transforming power of Christ.

Did John write the Gospel? In the context of writing of the time, that question has to be qualified by the further one of, in what sense write? But before discussing that further, let me say that I do not think it impossible that he could have sat down at a desk with writing materials and scratched away. Some have argued that John, a fisherman, could not have written the Greek of the Gospel. In the past, it has even been suggested that the Gospel was written in Aramaic first. The evidence for this seems very poor, and the theory is probably an attempt to overcome the apparent obstacle of a Galilean fisherman writing a Greek book.

Contemporary thought would incline to the view that Greek was more widely used and spoken amongst the people than had been previously thought. It is quite possible that the Septuagint, the Greek translation of the Jewish scriptures, was the edition used in Synagogues. Jesus' conversation with Pilate would presumably have been in Greek.

When we are thinking about a society that is very different from ours and, in particular, does not have the educational structure we understand, we should be cautious about making judgements on the intellectual and educational status of someone who is the son of a man who owns fishing boats. To conclude that such a person would be incapable of writing a book in Greek is little short of snobbish prejudice.

Furthermore, to argue that the book is too sophisticated to have been written by such a person is to make the often-repeated error of inferring that because something is unlikely it did not happen. It is unlikely that a patent clerk would be particularly good at physics but Albert Einstein was. One might not expect the son of a Warwickshire glovemaker to be particularly good at writing but William Shakespeare was. Why should not the son of a fisherman write the greatest Gospel?

Rowan Williams makes the point that the Greek of the Gospel is relatively simple, using a fairly limited vocabulary. He contrasts it with the more pompous Greek of Luke's Gospel which he likens to civil service writing. It also is different from the complicated expressions that Paul produces which one can imagine come from him dictating as he argues out his point with vigour to the walls of his cell. Williams goes on to say of the writing that, 'It's measured, it's careful, it's rhythmical and poetic. It's beautifully constructed, but it is extremely simple.'[1]

Certainly, some of the writing in the Gospel is superbly effective in its simple but graphic description. Some is like great poetry. Other parts seem complicated and repetitive.

However, I think it is unlikely that John toiled to make the letters appear on a manuscript. The epistles of Paul make it clear that even Paul who has a very direct link with at least some of the epistles did not himself form the letters on the page. He used a scribe, and we are even told his name in Romans. He adds his own personal message. Paul sometimes wrote a little at the end of the epistles (1 Cor 16:21; Gal 6:11; Col 4:18; 2 Thess 3:17). Paul draws attention to his own lack of skill in physically writing. It seems likely that Paul was dictating the contents of the letters and that the words are his. Is it likely that the Gospel is dictated by John?

It would seem strange that if he was writing a book in that way in which he featured as a central character he would use the language that is there. Would he not say such things as, 'I saw and believed,' rather than, 'He saw and believed'? (John 20:8).

I think we should consider that there is an author, someone other than John, who has composed the book. The author may well have used a scribe to write it, but the words are his, or hers. This author has remarkable literary skills for the Gospel contains some great writing, beautifully neat and dramatic descriptions. It also contains a great deal of repetition and at times a lack of organisation. In modern terms, there was no literary editor.

I am suggesting that the author is someone other than John not because I think that John would be incapable of writing it but because I think it provides the best explanation for the nature of the writing. A marked feature of the Gospel is the way in which there is repetition and at times a lack of orderly presentation. This has been taken by some to indicate multiple revisions and alterations. However, a suggestion that has been made in the past and seems to me most likely is that the author is creating a Gospel by listening to the teaching of the apostle.

One can imagine a church community grown up around the Apostle John, the disciple whom Jesus loved. It is important that his message that Jesus is the Christ and that faith in him gives life is spread. Someone is designated to put into writing the Gospel according to John. Rather than John dictating a book or most of it, the author puts down the sermons and lessons he has heard. This method of construction means that at times the author mixes up the teaching about Jesus which the Apostle is giving and teaching that the Apostle heard Jesus give. Quite probably this is because the author himself is unclear about the boundary between the two. I think that this is the best explanation of the fact that the Gospel contains all sorts of details and especially the way the disciples felt, but then sometimes makes the same point several times.

My hypothesis is, therefore, that the Apostle John centred his teaching on the core message that Jesus is the Christ and thus was following the general teaching of the very early church. His mission was to make that significant and meaningful to everyone. The person writing is someone who has heard this teaching and is therefore contemporary with John. It would seem sensible to me to presume that the majority of the Gospel was written during John's lifetime. There is a tradition that he lived to a great age but that is beside the point. The material is directly from his personal experience and not from the other Gospels. His teaching reflects his primary concern to get people to have faith in Jesus. So is it reasonable to think that John's Gospel is an early piece of writing?

Could John be early: external evidence

Although scholars have long argued that John's Gospel is a later work than the other three New Testament Gospels, the physical evidence, such as it is, does not correlate with this. Hill, in his excellent book *Who Chose the Gospels?*[2], examines the existing documentary evidence for the earliest Gospels. His book is concerned with the non-canonical Gospels, but nonetheless as he describes the earliest documentary evidence, it is quite evident that there are as many instances of fragments of John's Gospels as of any, and indeed it is Mark that seems to be missing to some extent. The earliest known codex, a binding of the Gospels in a book-like form, is of Luke and John. The oldest known fragment of any Gospel is a part of John's Gospel, the Rylands fragment.

One cannot draw much from this other than to say that it does not support a view that John was a later Gospel brought into the canon at a later date and with less authority. Indeed, in Hill's book, he demonstrates how from a very early stage in church history, there were considered to be four Gospels. John has a place as much as any.

Hill argues convincingly that Justin, writing in Rome around AD 150 knew John's Gospel. He quotes Jesus' saying about being born again and the subsequent argument of Nicodemus about entering his mother's womb again.[3]

He also quotes Eusebius who gives a description of how the apostle John was asked to write his Gospel. He suggests that he is in turn relating something that Papias said. Papias was probably born around AD 70. Hill comments that the claims made there are historically inaccurate, but they do indicate that this is an extremely early tradition. If there are these theories about how the Gospel came to be written and perhaps addressing the question of why it is so different from the other three which are in circulation in the early part of the first century, then it is not unreasonable to conclude that the Gospel itself had been around for some time.

The arguments about the age of different fragments of papyrus and the reliability and significance of references with the writings of early Christians form a large subject for scholarly debate, study and speculation. The conclusion I wish to stress is that this type of hard material evidence and what can be gleaned from the early writings of others does not support the idea that John's Gospel enters the scene at a later date. It is entirely possible from this point of view that John's Gospel is as old as any of the others.

Could John be early: internal evidence

Most of the views about the age and relationship of the Gospel to the history of Christianity arise from its content. However, I think that if we look at what the Gospel says and its priorities, there are good reasons for believing that it is an early document.

John's Gospel contains a lot of detail about times and places in comparison to the Synoptics. There are occasions when John gives a vague idea, using an expression of 'sometime later'. He also frequently describes events as occurring on the next day or after two days, for example, 'When the two days were over' (John 4:43), which may be a way of saying, 'a couple of days later' or 'a short time afterwards'.

However, John frequently associates particular parts of his account to Jewish festivals. The feeding of the five thousand was near Passover time (John 6:4). John has Jesus going on several occasions to Jerusalem, and quite sensibly, these are often for festivals. Thus the clearing of the temple was at Passover time (John 2:23), the healing at Bethesda was at an unspecified festival (John 5:1), Jesus teaches in the temple during the feast of Tabernacles (John 7), Jesus is nearly stoned in the temple precincts at the festival of Dedication (John 10:22) which the writer helpfully explains was in winter, and, of course, his arrest, trial and crucifixion are just before the Passover.

In relation to these festivals, two events are described as occurring on specific days. One is when he speaks in the temple and the temple police fail to, or perhaps lack the courage to, arrest Jesus (John 7:37), and the other is the anointing of Jesus at Bethany (John 12:1). When describing Andrew's and another disciple's first meeting with Jesus, we are even told the time of day (John 1:39).

Not only are there many details about times and dates, but he also gives specific place names. Apart from Jerusalem and areas such as Judea, Samaria and Galilee, there are specific locations, either towns or places within Jerusalem identified on 15 occasions (John 2:1; 2:12; 3:22; 4:5; 4:46; 5:2; 6:16; 6:59; 8:20; 11:1; 18:1; 18:15; 18:28; 19:13; 19:17). The tomb is identified as being near the place of crucifixion (John 19:41), and the final resurrection appearance is by the sea of Tiberias (John 21:1).

The towns and villages do not always tie up with current geographical knowledge. However, there is no reason to think that the author made up place names. What would be the point of that? The fact that we cannot identify them is more likely to reflect the way places' names do change and settlements alter so that what was the centre becomes a forgotten small area.

John contains lots of details. Some have tried to see in each and every one some representation of a theological concept. Common sense would suggest that John had these details and gives them because that is the way it was. It also suggests that the source of the Gospel is someone who was there, who remembered where it happened and when.

One intriguing circumstance is the account of Peter going to the High Priest's house after the arrest of Jesus. He goes with another disciple who is not named but was, we are told, known to the High Priest. The implication is that this is how Peter was able to enter the courtyard and get close to what was going on with ultimately heartrending consequences for Peter. It has been suggested that the reason the disciple is not named is that at the time of writing the situation was still dangerous. If the identity of the disciple was revealed, it could put him in a very difficult position. This is entirely speculative but worth mentioning as one possible reason for thinking that this Gospel was written early on.

Another strange reference in John's Gospel is to Bethlehem. Jesus was known as Jesus of Nazareth. That was his town. However, the idea that Jesus was born in Bethlehem clearly goes back a long way. Both Luke and Matthew give accounts of the birth, and both clearly state that Jesus was born in Bethlehem. Matthew explains the significance of this in terms of the prophecy of Micah. Luke gives an explanation of why Jesus was born in Bethlehem, the census, but does not explicitly state any other significance to the fact that this is where he was born. Matthew on the other hand gives no explanation as to why the family were in Bethlehem; it is not even suggested that they had travelled there. That it fulfils a prophecy is made clear, and then there appears to be an explanation of why they went eventually to Nazareth as though there had been no previous association with the town.

John does not give any birth narrative at all. However, there is described a discussion going on amongst people who were following Jesus and trying to decide on his significance. In Chapter 7:40–44 the dilemma is described. People believe that the Messiah does not come from Galilee. Nazareth is in Galilee and thus Jesus of Nazareth comes from Galilee. Those involved in the controversy refer, without a specific reference, to the scripture saying that the Messiah comes from Bethlehem. Thus the concept referred to by Matthew is echoed. What is curious is that the Gospel makes no further comment on the problem. There is no reference to the belief that Jesus was born in Bethlehem. The dispute is not resolved or put into context. All we are told is that some people found that the lack of a link to Bethlehem was a barrier to believing Jesus was the Messiah whereas it was not to others.

Could it be that the Gospel was written before it was widely known that Jesus was born in Bethlehem? It might be argued that it was written at a time when it was so well known that Jesus was born in Bethlehem that it was unnecessary to explain that. But is that the style of the writer? This Gospel contains lots of explanations about traditions, normal practice, and why things were said and done. To make no comment whatsoever on the irony of the discussion if it is so well known that Jesus was born in Bethlehem seems odd. The curiosity of the passage outweighs any clear conclusion, but I suggest it inclines to an early writing rather than a late.

Eucharist

One of the greatest of mysteries and peculiarities of John's Gospel relates to the institution of the Lord's Supper. John quite amazingly does not contain the description of the episode described in the Synoptics where at the last meal he shared with his disciples, he takes bread and wine and tells them to see these as symbols of his sacrifice and, furthermore, commands them to repeat the ritual. This is one event in the life of Jesus for which we have evidence, an account, outside the Gospels; that is to say Paul's account which we have mentioned earlier. Why does John not include it? This is a very remarkable fact. If John's Gospel was written after the others and with knowledge of them, why would the writer leave out this important instruction? It is not as though the Last Supper as a meeting is excluded; it occupies chapters 13 to 17. There are also the words of 6:50–56 which seem to be the very words of the association between Christ's death and the symbols of bread and wine. What is missing is the clear instruction for the memorial and thereby the institution of a regular ritual involving the symbolism of bread and wine. To me, this is strong evidence for the early nature of the Gospel. To omit this central part of Christian life once it had become established practice seems really peculiar.

My suggestion is that the book was written before it was a well-established practice. Once the formal re-enactment of this highly significant instruction had become part of the established practice of Christian churches then it would be bizarre to omit it from the narrative. So many of the details of the arrest and trial of Jesus are presented in both the Synoptic and Johannine Gospels that some explanation is required for the omission of the Eucharist.

One has to remember that the instruction from Jesus was not 'when you have church services you must include a ceremony that reproduces the simple actions I have performed and the words I have uttered about them.' Matthew and Mark exclude the instruction to repeat the symbolism as a memorial. There are variations in the wording of the crucial words of institution between ancient texts of Luke's Gospel. Paul's account clearly has the instruction to associate the memory with repetition. It could be argued that Jesus is telling them to remember him every time they break bread and drink wine rather than develop a special ceremony. If the Lord's supper had not become an established form of service by the time John was teaching and the Gospel was being written, then there might be good reasons for this particular memory to be excluded.

We know that at an early stage in the Church's history, there were rumours running around that this new sect ate human flesh and drank blood. A good example of this is in the letter written by Pliny the Younger to the Emperor Tiberius in about AD 112. This is about Christians and refers to his discoveries on their practices. They gathered together for a meal, 'but of an ordinary sort' (Epistulae X 96). Surely this is an allusion to the theory that Christians performed these cannibalistic rituals. Is it not quite likely that at a relatively early stage in church development concerns about how Jesus' words were being interpreted led to a situation where caution was needed when talking about the Eucharist? John does not mention the meal explicitly, perhaps to avoid arousing suspicions, perhaps because there was a view that it was a practice best avoided, perhaps that it was secret.

However, John does not omit this profound imagery, altogether. He does report Jesus as saying, "The bread which I shall give is my own flesh" (John 6:51), and, "Whoever eats my flesh and drinks my blood has eternal life, and I will raise him up on the last day" (John 6:54). In this way, John does follow the teaching of Jesus by drawing attention to these words and the use of the images of bread and the true vine as images of Jesus. I suggest John is tactfully avoiding a statement that people should have a ceremony in which bread and wine are declared to represent the flesh and blood of Christ. He could do this because this was not yet seen as an established practice. Paul's letter to Corinth indicates that people were interpreting the practice in different ways, hence Paul's need to give instruction on what he thought was appropriate. At the time Paul was writing to Corinth, the church had not yet fully established a clear routine on this matter. John's Gospel could be a contemporary or even earlier document. Paul gives instructions about not eating or drinking too much and sharing. John avoids the ritual meal completely.

Chronology

How should we view the very different chronology of events that we find in John's Gospel compared to the Synoptics? It is often argued that John has distorted the story so that he can create his book based around a series of signs. I wish to argue that the more complicated timeline is in fact evidence of the prior nature of John's Gospel. The chronology in John is messy. I suggest that is because it just happened that way. There is no subtle symbolism. Is it not more likely that the synoptic tradition has condensed the events into one neat pattern that fits a simplified account of Jesus' life? It all neatly builds to a climax with a final period in Jerusalem culminating in the arrest, trial, crucifixion and resurrection.

Sometimes in John's Gospel, there is a great deal of precision about dates and the relation of events to Jewish festivals, at others, there is considerable vagueness. Three separate Passover festivals are identified making Jesus' ministry over at least two years, but it is clear that some periods of time are of an unspecified length, and it is possible that a whole year was spent in one area for which we are given no details. However, the story reads as though Jesus begins his ministry at the wedding in Cana, which was apparently shortly before the Passover and then, of course finishes at the Passover which would be two years later.

John unequivocally has Jesus' ministry overlapping with John the Baptist's in contradiction to the Synoptics. Mark very firmly says, 'After John had been arrested, Jesus came into Galilee proclaiming the Gospel of God' (Mark 1:14). Matthew also states that Jesus' ministry begins after the arrest of John. Luke is less specific about the timing and does not indicate it as the trigger for the start of Jesus' ministry, but he does report Herod's arrest of John before he starts the account of Jesus' ministry. John, on the other hand, states quite clearly that Jesus was with his disciples in Judea and that John was there also (John 3:22).

Why should John give this different account of the timing of the two ministries? Does it not make more sense to say that the synoptic writers want to emphasise the distinction between the teaching of John and what Jesus said and did. Jesus comes after and does something on a totally different level. John was the herald, the forerunner and like the prologue to the play leaves the stage before the real action begins. John's Gospel, however, gives us the events as they happened without any particular motive.

John's account begins as Jesus appears at the Jordon in Judea where John is baptising and is himself baptised by John. Here he gathers some of his first disciples including Peter, Andrew and Philip (although Peter is a Galilean. There seems to be considerable uncertainty about the place Bethsaida from where John says they come). He then goes into Galilee and visits Cana and Capernaum.

Then we are told it is the Passover, and Jesus goes to Jerusalem. This is the occasion when he clears the temple. He subsequently meets Nicodemus. Following this, Jesus goes into Judea and with his disciples is baptising people.

Jesus leaves Judea and goes through Samaria, encountering the woman by the well but finally reaches Galilee. 'Later on' (uncharacteristically vague) he goes to Jerusalem for a festival, not specified, and heals the man at the pool of Bethesda. 'Some time later' he is back in Galilee. It is near the time of the Passover (so a whole year after clearing the temple) and he feeds the five thousand. We are told he stayed in Galilee and wanted to avoid Judea. However, he does go in secret to the Festival of the Tabernacles. (Sukkot—end of September / early October) He heals a man and tells him to wash in the pool of Siloam, which is in Jerusalem.

The narrative suddenly announces that it is winter, and the festival of Dedication (Hanukkah—late November to late December). Jesus is in Jerusalem. Having angered the Jews, he withdraws to across the Jordan and then goes to Bethany for the raising of Lazarus. We are told quite specifically that it is just under two miles from Jerusalem. Following the attention that this caused, he withdraws to the edge of the desert, to Ephraim (30 km northeast of Jerusalem, now called Taybeh). He stays there with his disciples until the Passover. There is speculation about whether he will show himself again in Jerusalem.

The final part of the story now begins, and the scene is set as we are told it is now the Passover again and Jesus goes to Bethany. Jesus enters Jerusalem riding a donkey and to adulation from the crowd. Whilst in Jerusalem, he is arrested, tried and crucified. There are the resurrection appearances in Jerusalem and then the final one by the sea of Tiberias.

There are thus apparently five different visits to Jerusalem described. In the Synoptics, only one visit is given. His repeated visits make one detail more straightforward. The place for the Last Supper has been identified and arranged by Jesus before his disciples go to prepare the Passover meal. In the Synoptics, it is then something of a mystery how Jesus has arranged this and who his contacts are. In John's Gospel, it is nothing very remarkable.

John Robinson makes a lot of interesting points about the chronology and argues, I think, very convincingly, that the synoptic chronology is compatible with John. There are a number of strong arguments as to why the cleansing of the temple makes sense at the beginning of the ministry rather than a few days before the crucifixion. If these events were so recent, why were they not mentioned at the trial?

The difference in dates and times reaches its most dramatic distinction from the Synoptics over the date of the crucifixion and with it the Last Supper. The Synoptics are unequivocal that the Last Supper was the Passover meal and thus the Pesach began at dusk on the Thursday evening. Whereas John tells us that the Friday, Good Friday, was the day of preparation and that the Passover began on the Sabbath, the Saturday. The evening meal at which Jesus washes the disciples' feet and which ends with the arrest is described as, 'It was before the Passover festival' (John 13:1). When Jesus is taken to Pilate, the Jews stay outside to avoid defilement so that they can eat the Passover meal (John 18:28). We are told that 'because it was the eve of the Passover', the Jews did not want the bodies to remain on the cross for the coming Sabbath 'since that Sabbath was a day of great solemnity' (John 19:31). The body of Jesus is laid in a tomb that was 'near at hand and it was the eve of the Jewish Sabbath' (John 19:42). There can be no avoiding the fact that as far as John is concerned, the Passover was the Friday evening to Saturday evening whereas the Synoptics following Mark have the Passover meal as the one shared by Jesus with his disciples on the Thursday evening.

What conclusions should we draw from these differences? Those who see John's Gospel as secondary, see these as examples of disregard for accuracy in the pursuit of his particular agenda. But what agenda is enhanced by this version? The timing emerges repeatedly in the course of explaining other details. There is no association with any other symbolism. It fits no particular theme or theology. As a detail, it contributes nothing to the story to change it from the Synoptics if that is what John has done.

However, is it not more likely that John gives this chronology because that is how it was? There are obvious, very powerful reasons for aligning the Last Supper with the Passover meal. Jesus becomes the Paschal lamb. It makes a very telling and significant theological point. When the two events occurred so close together, it is not difficult to imagine that popular culture merged the two even if it was not a deliberate adjustment by a Gospel writer. It makes no sense to suggest that John had seen the Synoptics and was aware of their view of the relationship between the crucifixion and the Passover and yet decides to state that it is different.

I suggest that this fact alone is a powerful argument in support of the view that John was written without knowledge of the Synoptics; that it was composed before them. I can see no sensible value in changing historical facts to disassociate the two events, and so it seems to me far more likely that John has the historical truth and that for one reason or another the Synoptic Gospels have merged the two.

The whole drama of the final days in Jerusalem as portrayed in the Synoptics makes a fitting climax to the account of the life, death and resurrection of Jesus. John's account does not convey some added meaning by saying that Jesus went several times to Jerusalem. I think it was simply because that is what happened.

It is not only plausible but the most likely explanation of the way the story is told that the Gospel is an early version of the Christian message. There is nothing in the external evidence we have to contradict that, and there are several issues within the Gospel itself which can most simply be explained by this position. This links to the concept stated in the Gospel itself that it is the testimony of an individual who was a close personal friend of Jesus. I think that John is the person that is meant by the references to a disciple whom Jesus loved. The style of writing suggests that the apostle did not write the book himself but that somebody else put into written words what John was saying and teaching. John was not dictating in the way that Paul probably created his letters. It would make sense if the author was putting down what John was uttering, not just to the writer, but to a group of people probably as teaching or sermons. Thus some topics are revisited, and there is a blurring of the margins between what Jesus was heard to say and what Jesus was understood to be saying.

References

1. Rowan Williams, *An introduction to St John's Gospel*, St Paul's Theological Centre, Saturday 17th January 2009
   http://rowanwilliams.archbishopofcanterbury.org
2. C E Hill, C E (2010) *Who Chose the* Gospels, Oxford: Oxford University Press.
3. Ibid p136

Chapter 6
Jesus Speaks

Some commentators would have us believe that virtually nothing in John's Gospel is a faithful representation of Jesus' words. This is partly because of the general approach to the Gospel but also because of the way Jesus appears to speak. If one thing stands out above all the other differences from the Synoptic Gospels, it is the way Jesus speaks. The style of talking and the content are different. In John's Gospel, Jesus speaks of himself in terms that we do not find elsewhere, and Jesus himself is found asserting his divine authority. Those who would see this Gospel as more removed from the historical Jesus would take these speeches to be inauthentic. To them, they represent a creation by the author to say things about Jesus which may well be true but were never uttered by Jesus himself.

That the words of Jesus in John's Gospel are different is blatantly obvious, but what is the authentic voice of Jesus? What would we have heard if we had been with him by the Sea of Galilee, in the streets of Jerusalem, or in the more private discussions amongst his followers? We do not have a sound recording nor a shorthand reporter's notes. How have the words of Jesus come to be represented in the Gospels?

There are a few examples where it does seem that the Gospel writers have attempted to give us the precise utterance. The most clear-cut are the cases where an Aramaic word is inserted.

Jesus raises the daughter of Jairus with the words, 'Talitha cum' (Mark 5:41). There can be no question but that this is meant to be exactly what Jesus said, what we would have heard had we been there. Likewise in the description of the healing of the deaf and dumb man, the Aramaic word, 'Ephphatha' is given (Mark 7:32–35).

Matthew and Luke in their account of the raising of Jairus' daughter do not give the Aramaic word but instead just give the translation. Thus they describe Jesus performing the miracle in just the same way, sending most of the people away, taking the girl by the hand and telling her to arise but without the detail of the exact word used. The point is that if we consider Mark's version an exact description of the words used by Jesus, then Matthew and Luke's version is also that apart from the fact that they have translated it into Greek. So how much else of the words of Jesus are in fact given to us as exact recollections albeit in Greek rather than Aramaic?

Translation is not an exact science. Sometimes it is fairly easy to put a word or expression into another language with exactly the same sense and range of meaning. Mark gives the translation of 'Talitha cum' which Luke gives without the Aramaic. However, even here there is a difference. Luke and Mark use the same Greek word for arise but different words to address the girl herself. There is probably no significance in this, but it simply underlines the point that the translator has to exercise choice and interpretation. There is no great theological point or matter of spiritual significance in the words Jesus used to tell the girl to get up, but elsewhere in the Gospel, the transmission of Jesus' uttered expression into Greek writing has inevitably involved a more complex process than a simple computerised translation.

There is one other particular example of the attempt to give us the precise words used by Jesus as a 'sound memory' and that is some of the words on the cross. Matthew's Gospel has Jesus saying, "Eli, Eli, lema sabachthani" (Matthew 27:46), and Mark, "Eloi, Eloi, lema sabachthani" (Mark 15:34). It is often said that 'Eli' is Hebrew and 'Eloi' is Aramaic, but it seems that the words, as we have them, do not fit neatly with either language. Of course, all we have is a transcription in Greek letters of what was said in another language which has a different script. More significantly, part of the point of the whole episode is that the people listening were not sure just what was said. It is hardly surprising that Jesus being tortured to death was not able to express himself clearly. Some thought he had said, "Elijah," someone that he had asked for a drink.

The uncertainties about just what Jesus said and whether he was quoting the start of the 22nd psalm are apparently so controversial that the Gospel writers have left the question open and given us what details they have. This is their motive for including as closely as possible what was heard. Why Mark chooses to give us the Aramaic words in the two miracles is another question, but for the most part, the Gospel writers have given us a Greek translation.

One can suppose that individuals who had short meetings with Jesus, episodes that would have been a moment in a lifetime, would have very vivid memories of the time and a recollection of the words used. I suggest that individuals vary in just how well they can remember precisely what was said on a particular occasion. I think for the most part, people overestimate their ability. As I look back in my life at the most important moments when people imparted highly significant things to me, I can recollect the scene, picture it in my mind and remember what was given to me, but in all honesty, I am not sure if I can truly remember the precise words and moreover the sentence formation.

What does seem likely is that the more surprising, the more puzzling and enigmatic things that Jesus said are more likely to be remembered exactly. Thus in the story of the healing of the woman with haemorrhages, Jesus says, "Who touched me?" (Mark 5:30), or perhaps "Who touched my clothes?" Even here, there is room for uncertainty. In either version the remark is memorable because it is peculiar given that he was surrounded by a crowd pressing around him.

A more disturbing example is the incident with the Syro-Phoenician woman (Mark 7:25–30). The apparently harsh words of Jesus speaking of giving the children's food to the dogs is so different from what we find elsewhere in the kindness and openness of Jesus that it stands out. These words, or some very close to them, must be what was heard. What this story does not give us is the context of the whole conversation. Was there a twinkle in Jesus' eye as he said it? The woman was not put off by his words and indeed gave a sharp, witty reply. I suggest Jesus knew the personality before him and never intended not to help the woman.

Indeed, most of Jesus' conversations must have been far more extensive than what is recorded in the Gospels. All we have is a short extract and particularly in Mark, this briefest and most abrupt of the Gospels. When Zacchaeus encountered

Jesus, was the conversation really confined to the few sentences that are recorded or have we been given a summary? It is surely likely that in almost every instance of a recorded conversation a great deal more was said than is put in the Gospel.

The parables were probably told with a great deal more elaboration than we have. Was Jesus not a good storyteller? He certainly was very successful at holding his audience's attention. He was apparently a popular dinner guest; no doubt his conversation was captivating and entertaining.

We are told that people found his teaching astounding and authoritative. Whilst we may appreciate the clear pronouncements that are recorded, the teaching as it appears in the Gospels does not seem something likely to captivate crowds nor to take very long. The Sermon on the Mount is generally considered to be a collection of Jesus' sayings, and it is surely very likely that with teaching, Jesus repeated the same stories and sayings on several occasions. What good teacher would not? If we accept that the account of Jesus' teaching on the hillside is not a transcript of a speech he gave, then we should also consider that throughout the Gospels, his teaching is not necessarily a precise historical representation of his words on a particular occasion.

With these thoughts in mind, we can turn to John's Gospel and try and understand what we have been given here. A feature of John's Gospel is the conversations. There are several relatively long encounters with individuals that are recorded in more detail than we find in the Synoptics. The conversation with the Samaritan woman by the well is the clearest example.

Dodd in his influential book *The Interpretation of the Fourth Gospel*[1] makes the startling comment that this cannot be genuine as there were no witnesses. But a major feature of the whole episode is that the woman went and started telling lots of people about Jesus and what he said. There seems good reason to think that this was a personal encounter which made a huge impression and was recounted and retold many times. It is of significance that one feature is an enigmatic, teasing comment from Jesus at the beginning. He makes the comment about the idea that she should ask him for water knowing full well that she will not understand. It starts the dialogue, and this seems to be a technique Jesus used.

Napoleon famously is supposed to have said on the retreat from Moscow, "From the sublime to the ridiculous is a small step." In John's Gospel, we find Jesus often moves swiftly from the ridiculous to the sublime. I suggest a good example of this is the encounter with Nicodemus. It starts with one of these peculiar sounding, slightly humorous remarks. Jesus speaks of being born again. This has become such a frequently repeated phrase in Christian speaking and writing that it can easily be forgotten that when Jesus first said it, the comment was bizarre and incomprehensible. Jesus did not expect Nicodemus to understand, but it certainly started the discussion. This seems to be the way Jesus started conversations, and again we appear to have something authentic and characteristic of Jesus.

The problem with this conversation is, where does the historical description end and where does the theological teaching of the author commence? For just as it seems very plausible that Jesus did actually tell Nicodemus he had to be born again, did he really describe God's action of salvation in the famous words of 3:16, "God loved the world so much that he gave his only Son, that everyone who has faith in him may not die but have eternal life." What seems to be different is that Jesus is referred to in the third person whereas he usually uses the first person. That is not to say that this much-loved sentence is not an accurate representation of something Jesus said, but the phrasing has been changed so that it sounds like a commentary from the evangelist. Thus it could be a rephrasing of Jesus' words on this occasion, on another occasion or the testimony of John considering that it encapsulates the message of the entire book.

Do we conclude that when Jesus is referred to in the third person that these are not his words? I think not. In the Synoptic Gospels we find Jesus referring to himself by titles such as 'the Son of Man'. Thus in Mark's Gospel (Mark 9:31), we find that he is telling them, "The Son of Man is now to be given up into the powers of men, and they will kill him, and three days after being killed, he will rise again." What we have are at least two independent sources describing Jesus speaking about himself in the third person. It is reasonable to conclude that this is something he did at times.

What is more perplexing is what expressions did he use to speak of himself? The Son of Man seems to be the preferred title in the Synoptics but in John we find a wider range. 'Son of Man' is there and so is 'Son of God', but often it is simply 'the Son' in relation to God, the Father. I suggest that a key problem for the Gospels and particularly for John is to understand and convey the nature of the Christ. What is the relationship between Jesus and God?

It is not a simple question, and it never has been. At the time the Gospels were written, there must have been a complex confusion about the nature of divinity. Roman emperors, irrespective of their brutal behaviour, were called gods. The mythology of Greece and Rome, with stories of beings able to disguise themselves as human yet capable of good and awful actions, were far removed from the Jewish or Christian sense of God. These stories included the notion of beings who were father or mother, sometimes in the most bizarre circumstances, to other beings with a variety of divine or mortal conditions. In this context, how do you explain to the Roman and Greek world that there is one God and there is Jesus who is not like any other human being and has a special relationship to God? The teachers, preachers and writers of the early church had an immense problem as they sought to understand it and then explain it to others.

It is therefore not surprising that we find so many different forms of words. It also makes sense that Jesus himself was very cautious about anyone using any particular label.

I firmly believe that Jesus did use the expression 'Son of Man', especially because it was enigmatic. The expression, 'Son of Man' occurs in the Book of Daniel, but I do not believe he was relying on some pre-existing notion of a relationship to the divine arising from this. This seems to be such a small detail and too abstruse to be the explanation. However, many have stated that this is its origin. I suggest that Jesus used it as a neutral way of referring to himself which did not carry immediate associations for his listeners.

Equally I think it unlikely that this was the only term he used about himself. John's Gospel contains lots of teaching about the relationship between Jesus and God the Father. Is this all commentary by John? I think not all of it. I think that Jesus did refer to God as Father. It seems to be one important message that he imparted to his followers. His teaching of prayer begins, 'Our Father…' There is the tradition that he taught his disciples to consider God as 'Abba, Father'. As said earlier, there is some uncertainty about all this but it is something Paul repeated.

Surely therefore, it is highly likely that Jesus at times talked about what he was doing and what was happening in terms of the Father-Son relationship. Therefore if he did at times refer to himself in this way, then it is possible that any of these statements could be his precise words. On the other hand, it seems likely, as I have suggested earlier, that the Gospel is formed for a significant part from the teaching of John. Consequently some of these crucial statements are therefore the testimony of John, the disciple whom Jesus loved and perhaps the human to whom he was closest.

Matthew's Gospel does contain a passage very reminiscent of John in the way Jesus speaks about himself (Matthew 11:25), "I thank thee, Father, Lord of heaven and earth, for hiding these things from the learned and wise, and revealing them to the simple. Yes, Father, such was thy choice. Everything is entrusted to me by my Father, and no one knows the Father but the Son and those to whom the Son may choose to reveal him." It is an unusual type of comment to find in Matthew's Gospel, and one wonders how it comes to be incorporated. It certainly sounds very like the type of statement we find in John.

There are passages in the Synoptics which sound to be particularly relevant to the struggling infant church. Words that speak about the persecution of the early preachers such as the instructions for travelling preachers found in Matthew 10:17–23. Are these sayings simply a record of an utterance of Jesus or are they, at least to some extent, an encouragement inserted into the narrative given the authority of being spoken by Jesus?

What I think we should conclude is that in all the Gospels, we have the issue of which words are a simple Greek translation of the very words spoken by Jesus, which are to a smaller or greater degree a paraphrase of his words and which are sentiments that the writer firmly believed were true but are put into Jesus' mouth although there was no record of him actually uttering them. This is not a simple problem and no one can delineate with any certainty.

Furthermore, if I am correct in suggesting that John's Gospel originates from the testimony of John, the disciple whom Jesus loved, it is possible that they had many private discussions which gave John such a wealth of expressions and ideas that he himself may have forgotten what he came to understand and what he actually heard. The structure of the speeches and dialogue we find in John's Gospel is unlikely to be historically accurate. Jesus did not say all those things in that order and that particular time. However, it is equally unlikely that Jesus sat on a hillside and delivered the Sermon on the Mount. The conversations we find in the Synoptics are likely to be extremely brief summaries of all that was said. Even more so, the parables were no doubt told in a great deal more detail and, of course, probably with considerable variation when they were told on different occasions.

John's Gospel should not be considered any less a reliable source of the words of Jesus than any of the other Gospels. The Synoptics contain sayings that seem particularly relevant to the new church and its struggles with persecution. Are these all exactly what Jesus said and then selected by the Gospel writer for their relevance? Chapter 13 of Mark's Gospel is a case in point. There is as much reason for believing that some of Jesus words in the Synoptics are projections of early church teaching into his mouth as anything in John's Gospel.

Indeed, as suggested earlier, it is perfectly possible that John had heard Jesus say a great many things in lots of different circumstances. Consider for example, a conversation amongst the disciples about the passage in Genesis where Abraham is about to sacrifice Isaac. Someone points out that in the end he did not have to kill his own son. "But" says Jesus, "God's love for the world is such that he will do that." Thus when preaching, John recalls this and tells his hearers, "God so loved the world that he gave his only Son so that everyone who believes in him may not perish but have eternal life. Yes, I heard this from the Lord myself." The writer then incorporates that into the Gospel.

This is entirely fanciful, but it makes the point that we simply cannot know to what extent we are hearing the words of Jesus. If we believe that the Holy Spirit was inspiring those that compiled the Gospels, then we can have faith that they have recorded the truth that Christ wanted to impart.

Amen

There is one word ascribed to Jesus that we can have considerable confidence we would have heard him say, 'Amen.' There are many differences between the Synoptic Gospels and John, but one similarity is that they both record that Jesus began some of his most important sayings with, 'Amen.' (Luke appears to have translated the word rather than using the transliteration of the original Aramaic or Hebrew word.[2]) In John, it is repeated, Amen, amen, and occurs no less than 23 times.

Whereas the expression was well known as a means of affirming someone else's statement, in much the way that we use it, Jesus quite distinctively uses it for his own pronouncements. The Christian church used 'Amen' to affirm its teaching in the way we would expect, at the end of prayers and statements. We see this in Paul's letters. It must have been a particular feature of Jesus' teaching that he used it in this different way, that is to start a statement.

It tends to highlight statements of particular spiritual significance, but this is not its only use. In contrast, it is also the opening word that Jesus uses when telling his disciples that one of them is to betray him (John 13:21) and also his warning to Peter that he will disown him (John 13:38). As such it is therefore not simply a marker of a saying to be noted by the church as something to be considered carefully for spiritual development. It seems to be a way of highlighting an important statement.

With that in mind, it is of some interest to consider where it is not found. It does not occur in the passage often referred to as the High Priestly Prayer, Chapter 17 of the Gospel, which seems to contain a great deal of important sayings of spiritual significance, and it does not precede any of the 'I am' sayings. That seems particularly important. These sayings are surely of the greatest significance and yet this hallmark underlining is absent.

Thus the 'Amen' opening is something we find in the Synoptics and frequently quoted in John in a number of different types of situations. This seems to be an authentic feature of Jesus' speech. Should we see the sayings preceded by Amen, amen as more directly a quotation of Jesus than some others? That would suggest that the 'I am' sayings are perhaps not words of Jesus himself.

I do not think we can use it as a simple discriminator. There are some sayings in John which seem less likely to be direct quotations that do have the 'Amen' beginning, for example, when talking about the dead hearing the voice of the Son of God (John 5:25) and also some sayings that seem likely to be authentic which do not, for example, "Destroy this temple and in three days I will raise it up again" (John 2:19), something that was apparently quoted in his trial before the Jewish Council (Mark 14:58). Given that we are relying on personal recollection and people will remember that that is how Jesus often started his words, then it would not be surprising if there is some confusion about exactly when it was used.

Tyndale's beautiful English translation, 'Verily, verily I say unto you,' is a brilliant translation of the commanding authority of these words. All modern translations have failed to match it and perhaps they would have been better to revert to the original Greek word 'Amen'. In modern terms, I am reminded of the way in which the American Military are portrayed as beginning their public address messages with the expression, 'Now hear this'.

Parables

One of the very distinctive features of the way Jesus taught that is given prominence in the Synoptic Gospels is the use of parables. All three Gospels draw attention to it and, for example, Mark says, 'With many such parables he would give them his message, so far as they were able to receive it. He never spoke to them except in parables; but privately to his disciples he explained everything' (Mark 4:33–34). Not only is the style of teaching emphasised, but there are many examples given. This seems to be a major difference from John's Gospel. The parables are missing and so is the image of Jesus teaching extensively in this way. Why should this be?

The situation is more complicated than simply saying that John does not mention the parables. In fact, in two places in John's Gospel, he does refer to this sort of teaching. One is where Jesus speaks about the gate to the sheepfold and the other when he is describing the good shepherd as contrasted to the hired hand in Chapter 10. There is also the occasion when as part of the final discourse to the disciples in Chapter 16, Jesus says that he has been using a way of speaking which is not plain words. In both instances, John chooses to use a word that is different from the word we find so frequently in the Synoptic Gospels. They refer to *parabolos* (παραβολῆς) which is routinely translated everywhere as parables. John describes the sayings as a form of speech designated by the Greek word *paroimian* (παροιμίαν). Different translations of the Bible have given different translations of the word John uses. The New English Bible and REB actually use the word 'parable' in Chapter 10 but 'figure of speech' in Chapter 16, whilst other versions use some different expressions.

Are we meant to deduce some significance from John's use of a different word? It is possible that he saw parables as something rather different from the way Matthew, Mark and Luke did or that he thought his examples were not quite the same thing. However, it is surely more likely that there is no importance whatsoever to his use of a different word.

Given that John does not give any other explicit examples of the parables as we know them, it seems highly unlikely he was trying to draw a distinction and that in all probability he simply used a different word without any intention of drawing any distinction whatsoever. Indeed, if my view is correct that he had not seen any of the Synoptics, then there may well be no significance at all in his choice of word and it merely serves to reinforce the independent nature of this Gospel.

We have become so used to the concept of the parables and that this was an important part of Jesus' teaching style that it is easy to overlook the fact that the word 'parable' in the Synoptic Gospels encompasses very different styles of speaking. There are stories such as the Good Samaritan and the Prodigal Son which have a clear plot and some detail in them. And then, on the other hand, sayings like, "The kingdom of heaven is like a mustard seed," which is not a story but simply a stated allegory.

The verses which open chapter 10 (John 10:1–5) about a sheepfold have an allegorical character. John is definitely being allegorical here! It is easy to view this as in essence a story. A man breaks into a sheepfold by climbing over the wall. However, the sheep will not follow the thief who is trying to steal the sheep and follow the shepherd instead when he enters the fold as usual by the proper entrance. This could well be a parable in the sense with which we are familiar from the Synoptic Gospels.

Having explained that it was a 'parable', using his word, John then tells us that 'they did not understand what he meant by it' (John 10:6). The Synoptics tell us that people tended not to understand the parables. If, as I have suggested, the Gospel is based on preaching by John, then it would not be at all surprising if he took a parable and expounded on it. The Gospel then, partly for fear that we like Jesus' audience might not understand the parable, gives us the Apostle's interpretation and teaching rather than the simple story.

As part of this narrative, Jesus says, "I am the door of the sheepfold" (John 10:7). It is given the exalted status of being heralded by 'Amen, amen.' This, however, seems to be the interpretation of the allegorical account just given. Jesus is the door, 'those who have come before' are the thieves and robbers. Who are the ones who came before? In other contexts, one might think of the prophets, but surely that is not the intended association. There is no satisfactory explanation to this. If it were part of a sermon being delivered by John, then one could imagine that the failure of the law and its exponents in the Pharisees are being contrasted to the lifegiving role of Christ. The switching between allegory or metaphor and explicit statement is complex. Thus, "The thief comes only to steal, to kill, to destroy;" is allegorical but then, "I have come that men may have life, and have it in all its fullness" (John 10:10) is explicit.

What follows, the good shepherd and the hireling (John 10:12–13), seems to be really another parable with a very similar but different structure. Again the interpretation and the story seem mixed up. Now the comparison is between a true shepherd who stays with his sheep even in dangerous situations. The good shepherd lays down his life for his sheep. But so there is no doubt, it is made quite clear that Jesus is the good shepherd. The reference to the forthcoming passion is obvious, but this is said in the context of what a shepherd will do for his flock. This is contrasted with a temporary worker who runs away when a wolf appears.

Interpreting parables is something preachers have done for 2000 years and the way in which the Parable of the Sower is given a detailed explanation seems to suggest it goes back to the earliest of days. This section of the Gospel seems to include something of this sort.

Jesus' parables were, I think, often told as stories to make a point, and we make too much of their allegorical nature. We should not be trying to decode them. The message we should take away from the story about the door should perhaps be simply, you have to approach the truth face on; you cannot creep around.

The second story is more straightforward with the total commitment of Christ. It goes on into a passage (John 10:14–18) which does seem to be a message for the church. So it may be that a significant part of these words was not spoken by Jesus but John.

Leaving aside these two possible examples of parable stories in John's Gospel, there is the puzzling reference to parables in Jesus' final discourse to his disciples, "Till now I have been using *parables*; a time is coming when I shall no longer use *parables* but tell you of the Father in plain words" (John 16:25). When Jesus says this, to what is he referring? Is this meant to refer to the things said in this discourse or is it meant to refer more widely? And to what extent are we meant to construe the things that Jesus has been saying as figures of speech, something other than plain language. Jesus has been talking about going away and then returning. He has puzzled Thomas by saying that they know the way (John 14:5), and when he has spoken of going away for a little while, they ask, "What is this 'little while' that he speaks of? We do not know what he means" (John 16:18).

The passage comes to a climax when Jesus says that he is leaving the world again and going to the Father. The disciples respond, "Why, this is plain speaking; this is no *parable*" (John 16:28–29). So perhaps it is simply the talk about Jesus going away that is not plain. Perhaps this reference to a 'figure of speech' or 'parable' is no more than the contrast between an indirect reference to his forthcoming suffering and death and the clear statement that he is leaving the world and going to God. If so, then this is certainly a different sort of saying to those categorised as parables in the Synoptics.

So why does John not give us the parable stories with which we are so familiar from the Synoptics? John's Gospel centres on telling who Jesus is and how faith in him gives life. For the most part, the sayings of Jesus that he records are for that purpose. John does not give an account of Jesus' teaching about other matters. The parables in the Synoptics deal with a range of topics. Some are about Christian life, the way to treat other people, some about the way people respond to the kingdom of God. They are not repeated in John perhaps because this is not his central theme. Certainly, all the Gospels seem to recognise that the parables were often not understood by people hearing them. John is very concerned that we should understand everything. It may be that John is wary of including them as what he is doing is trying to make the Gospel plain to all. If the concept of the Gospel coming from listening to John's teaching is correct, then it may be that his teaching style was such that, either because he did not use them or that the emphasis was on the interpretation, the parables were not heard by the writer as a major element.

What the Gospels also tell us is that Jesus used direct language when talking to the disciples. This could be the crucial difference between the Synoptics and John. If John's Gospel is based on the witness of one of his closest disciples, then perhaps it is not surprising that what he gives us is the direct teaching he received from the Lord rather than the more illustrated teaching that was heard in public.

I am

One of the most distinctive features of John's Gospel is the 'I am,' sayings. They are unique to this Gospel, not occurring in the Synoptics or in the epistles: "I am the bread of life" (John 6:35); "I am the light of the world" (John 8:12); "I am the door" (John 10:7,9); "I am the good shepherd" (John 10:11,14); "I am the resurrection and the life" (John 11:25); "I am the way, the truth and the life" (John 14:6); and "I am the true vine" (John 15:1,5). They are sometimes seen as a specific group of seven special sayings. This is perhaps to make too much of a certain similarity.

The subjects and contexts are very different. One, the way, the truth and the life, is obviously three different things albeit related. There are also other sayings in the Gospel where Jesus begins, 'I am': "I am the one testifying in my own cause" (John 8:18); "I am of the world above" (John 8:23); and "Before Abraham was born, I am" (John 8:58). There are a number of other sayings in which Jesus puts himself at the centre of some statement, as for example when speaking to Pilate (John 18:37).

On the other hand, there are instances where one might have expected a similar phrase. When he speaks to the Samaritan woman, he talks of giving living water but does not say, 'I am the living water.' He does however, when talking of the Messiah say, "I am he" (John 4:26).

Jesus' conversation with the woman who asks for the living water, contrasts with Jesus' discussion with the crowd the day after the feeding of the five thousand. They too ask for what Jesus has described—in this case the bread that comes down from heaven and gives life to the world just as the woman asks Jesus for the water giving eternal life. However, to the crowd Jesus says, "I am the bread of life," but to the woman he changes the subject by asking about her husband.

In identifying himself with bread, of course, Jesus is also heard to be identifying himself with one of the two crucial elements of the Eucharist. John's Gospel does not contain the complementary saying about wine. "I am the true vine," is about something else altogether.

Our familiarity with these 'I am' sayings and the way in which they have such a special place in Christian tradition can make it difficult to appreciate the differences between them. When Jesus speaks of himself as the door and also as the good shepherd it is in the context of the closest, we get in John's Gospel to parables. It is as though Jesus is interpreting the parable and providing the analogy, the explanation. Here is an image of a sheepfold protecting sheep and the door as the means of securing access to them. Jesus identifies himself with that door. In the same way, we have another image of people tasked with looking after the sheep, but only the real shepherd is going to put the sheep's well-being before his own safety. Jesus tells us that he is that good shepherd.

The image of the true vine is another allegorical description. It does not come in conjunction with the features suggesting a story in the way we can easily imagine for the door and the shepherd, but nonetheless it is a very familiar and understandable concept. There is the fairly straightforward horticultural idea of a plant where the fruit develops on the branches but it is essential those branches are part of the whole plant. It is clearly allegorical and even has the further detail of the Father being the gardener. The allegorical nature is pushed even further with the idea of dead branches being thrown on the fire. One cannot help questioning whether this is preaching on the theme where the idea has been expanded to make points to the church. It is not difficult to imagine the preacher then looking at the congregation and challenging them, "Are you a dead branch?"

In these three sayings, we learn something about the nature of Jesus, his mission and how we should relate to him by illustration from very easily understood and familiar objects. Jesus is like a door; Jesus is like a good shepherd; Jesus is like a vine plant.

One cannot say the same about, "I am the resurrection and the life." The resurrection is not a concept that has the simple physical attributes and familiarity of the door, the shepherd and the vine. So what does it mean? Well, Jesus does go on to explain. Those who believe in him will have life beyond death. The statement is therefore far more than a metaphor. Jesus is not like the resurrection: Jesus himself is the means by which people can conquer death through faith in him. Linked in the same phrase is the central recurring theme of the Gospel: faith in Jesus gives life, the fundamentally different life that John wants us all to know.

Another recurring and fundamental theme of the Gospel is sight and light. It is no surprise therefore that we hear Jesus saying, "I am the light of the world." Whilst light is a familiar and easily understood concept, the assertion is not analogous. Jesus is not saying I am like a light, he is rather proclaiming that through him people can see and know the greatest truths. There is much more to be said about sight and light later on.

So where does, "I am the bread of life" fit in with this distinction between different sayings? On the one hand bread is definitely an everyday simple object, but on the other hand Jesus is saying that this is not ordinary bread but something which gives that central theme, life. Enigmatically, we have the statement, "Whoever comes to me shall never be hungry, and whoever believes in me shall never be thirsty" (John 6:35). But in this passage, there has been no mention of water, only bread. It ties in perfectly with what he has said to the Samaritan woman, but in a clumsy way we are left having to see the connection for ourselves.

One cannot escape the fact that imagery gets even more confused as the discourse continues about the bread of life. "I am the bread of life," is repeated (John 6:48) along with the comparison with manna. However, Jesus then says, "The bread which I will give is my own flesh" (John 6:51), and goes on to say that we are lifeless if we do not eat that flesh and drink his blood. There can be no doubt that this refers to the Eucharist. The passage repeats the importance of this and ends by tying it up again with the bread.

Here, surely, is a very good example of what sounds like preaching on a text. We start with the saying of Jesus that he is the bread of life, and the way in which we remember his sacrifice in eating bread and drinking wine is brought into the sermon. I suggest, therefore, that we have John relating something Jesus said to a crowd and then trying to explain what it means and linking it in with Communion.

There is no question of an allegorical character to the sayings in the final teaching before his arrest, "I am the way, I am the truth and I am life" (John 14:6). This is the assertion that Jesus himself is the way to know God and experience the special life in God. That Jesus says he is the life is, of course, a repetition of John's central theme. Faith in Jesus gives life. In a short while, the Gospel will be recounting the conversation between Pilate and Jesus where Jesus tells Pilate that his task is to bear witness to the truth. Do these three assertions belong together as something said one after another on a particular occasion by Jesus? We do not know. The distinction between John's teaching, John recounting things he has heard Jesus say, and his memory of a particular speech by Jesus is forever blurred. Perhaps it is like a painting where if you try and examine it closely, you will find the colours applied to the canvas have merged into each other, but when you stand back what you have is a clear and powerful image that truthfully conveys a scene.

References

1. Dodd, C H (1980) *The Interpretation of the Fourth Gospel*, Cambridge: Cambridge University Press, p450.
2. Dunn, James D G (2003) *Jesus Remembered*, Grand Rapids, Michigan: Eerdmans, p701

Chapter 7
Jesus Is Unique

The things that Jesus said form an important and large part of John's Gospel. They are central to the main objective of the Gospel which is to help people understand the unique and intimate relationship Jesus has with God and humankind. In addition to what was spoken, the Gospel adds to this by describing features of Jesus' personality and actions that support this view.

Jesus' insight into people's personality

One particular feature perhaps reflects the personal nature of the evangelist's testimony. This is his view that Jesus had a particular and great ability to understand and see into the personalities and thinking of the people he met. Early on in John's narrative, after Jesus has cleared the temple and he is in Jerusalem, the Gospel describes how many started to follow him. What follows in verses is pure commentary. John tells us that Jesus did not trust them. 'He knew men so well' (John 2:24). This is a great insight into the character of Jesus. The encounters we read about in John and the other Gospels seem to demonstrate a profound ability to understand what people are thinking, their motives and problems. Here John states this as an observation of his nature.

When Jesus speaks to the woman by the well, it emerges that he knows her personal circumstances (John 4:16). Jesus understands this woman, her life and her needs. It was a startling feature of the encounter and something she made a point of telling others, "a man who told me everything I have ever done" (John 4:29).

Another example is the healing of the man at the pool of Bethesda. The first thing that Jesus says to this man whose whole life is taken up with apparently waiting for a miraculous cure for his paralysis is, "Do you want to recover?" (John 5:6). The man does not answer the question but gives an excuse as to why he has never been cured. We are given no further details of the basis for the question, but it hints strongly at the important issue of empowering the patient to change from a passive sufferer to one who is actively seeking recovery. This is a universal issue as relevant today as it was 2000 years ago.

Even more tantalising is the second encounter with Jesus described in verse 14: "Leave your sinful ways or you may suffer something worse." No explanation of this remark is given at all. It may be that whoever witnessed it, perhaps the evangelist, had no idea. It serves no purpose other than to recall something that Jesus was heard to say. We do not learn this man's full story, but the description suggests Jesus understood and knew a great deal about this man's problems from a holistic point of view.

The encounter Jesus has with Nathaniel, which we find near the very beginning of the Gospel (John 1:44–51), is another instance of Jesus' knowledge of the person to whom he is speaking. There are other important elements to the story which I shall consider later when thinking about the central theme of seeing in this Gospel. However, at the heart of the story is Nathaniel's astonishment that Jesus knows his personality, and this is enhanced as Jesus promises that to Nathaniel will be given the privilege of seeing the glory of God.

Other examples of Jesus' insight into people's personality are to be found in the Last Supper when he announces the betrayal by Judas and Peter's forthcoming denial. Of course, Jesus may have been aware of what Judas had been up to with the Jewish authorities, but his prophecy about Peter demonstrates his knowledge of how Peter will react in a time of danger.

Miracles

All the Gospels highlight the fact that Jesus was set apart from ordinary people in that he had power to perform miracles. This special characteristic of Jesus is emphasised in John. If the parables are present in John only as a distant echo, the miracles are different. John clearly describes several miracles and a few seem to be the same episodes that we find in the Synoptics.

John describes seven specific miracles apart from the resurrection of Jesus and also not counting the large catch of fish at the resurrection appearance by the lake. John does, however, refer to other miracles with the description of them as signs. 'While he was in Jerusalem for Passover, many gave their allegiance to him when they saw the signs that he performed' (John 2:23). 'In spite of the many signs which

Jesus had performed in their presence, they would not believe in him' (John 12:37). There can be no doubt that John is referring to miracles of healing when he speaks of signs: 'A large crowd of people followed who had seen the signs he performed in healing the sick' (John 6:2).

This description of healing being a major and recurrent part of Jesus' ministry is similar to the testimony of the Synoptics. For example, Mark makes several references to the many miracles of healing that Jesus performed, 'He healed many who suffered from various diseases and drove out many devils' (Mark 2:34); 'For he cured so many that sick people of all kinds came crowding in upon him to touch him' (Mark 3:10). In contrast to the seven miracles in John's Gospel that are detailed, Mark describes nineteen specific miracles, if one includes the withering of the fig tree but not the transfiguration or the resurrection.

It is part of the general characteristic of the Gospel that more detail is given about each incident than we find in the Synoptics, so that although there are relatively few, they occupy a significant proportion of the text.

Thus, in John, we have: turning the water into wine (John 2:1f); the official's son (John 4:46f); the paralysed man at Bethesda (John 5:1f); the feeding of the five thousand (John 6:1f); walking on the water (John 6:16f), healing of the man born blind (John 9:1f) and the raising of Lazarus (John 11:1f). There can be little doubt that two of these, the feeding of the five thousand and walking on the water, are the same episodes as recounted in the Synoptics.

A question arises with regard to the healing of the royal officer's son. Is this story, the same episode as that described in Matthew (8:5) and Luke (7:1)? They describe healing at a distance the dependent of a senior figure. The Q source has a centurion in contrast to the officer in royal service in John. Luke has a servant, Matthew a boy, and John has a son as the patient. In Matthew and Luke, Jesus contrasts the faith of the centurion with a lack of faith by Jewish people.

In John's account, Jesus criticises people for wanting signs. "Will none of you ever believe without seeing signs and portents?" (John 4:48), which otherwise seems an odd comment to make to the desperate plea for help from a man terrified of losing his son. It seems peculiar that Jesus is initially reluctant to help. Perhaps though, Jesus is continually anxious that people may see him as a miracle worker. The Synoptics tell us how often he orders those healed not to tell others about it. This may be the dilemma that John is recording in this rather abrupt part of the narrative.

Turning water into wine

Given that there are relatively few miracles in John's Gospel, those that are there are some of the more dramatic and startling. None more so than the curious story of turning water into wine. Mostly miracles are about helping people in physical or mental distress. One might think that the needs of the hungry crowd in the mass feedings are not so serious a problem as the paralysed, blind and bereaved people that are recipients of most of the miracles we find in the Synoptic Gospels, but nonetheless it is addressing a real need for a lot of people Walking on the water seems just a matter of convenience to Jesus himself, but this act of munificence meets a curious need. The main problem is that the hosts of a wedding are embarrassed by a lack of wine to entertain the guests. One cannot feel that the guests will suffer through a lack of wine.

The account is filled with the details of the actions undertaken and then the resultant assessment of the wine. However, it is prefaced by the conversation between Jesus and his mother. Jesus seems to dismiss his mother's concerns and say that his hour has not come. What does this mean? There is no clear explanation. Even more curiously, his mother seems to anticipate that Jesus will help by instructing the servants to follow his directions.

It is not difficult to see why this odd miracle has been widely considered to be a sign. Of course, at the end we are told that it was the first sign by which Jesus revealed his glory. The theory that John's Gospel is a book of signs is off to a start. However, where is the associated theology? There is no accompanying statement of Jesus about his nature or mission. There is no further action that ties in with it. The next story is of Jesus clearing the temple. One can envisage some metaphor of bringing in a new regime, clearing out the old and pouring in new wine, but this is creative interpolation of a link. The story is not about turning old wine into new, clearing out of anything or bringing in something new. It is turning one fluid into another, and this is nothing like driving traders out of the temple. No such connection is suggested. There is nothing in the Gospel to join these actions together. The miracle stands alone without explanation and without any commentary. Many excellent sermons and clever theological writings have sought to demonstrate the link, but, in all honesty, common sense tells us that there is no link at all.

John does not leave a hidden trail of theological connection. He is careful to explain to his readership many aspects and details. He has just explained that 'Messiah' is the Hebrew word for 'Christ' (John 1:41). He explains many of the customs and practices of Jewish religion when necessary, and when there are links, they are made obvious. When Jesus cures a blind man, then we have him saying that "It is for judgement that I have come into this world—to give sight to the sightless and make blind those who see" (John 9:39); hardly a cryptic or obscure connection.

Those who are convinced that there is a hidden message in the Gospel will not be convinced, but I contend that there is no more significance intended than the remarkable power of Jesus in performing such an act.

Miracles are difficult for us in these days. We know the world to be ruled by laws, scientific laws that unlike imposed human laws cannot be broken. The scientific method demands that if an exception to the law exists then the law is invalid and must be revised to take into account the new observation. If it had turned out as some scientists believed a few years ago that they had observed neutrinos travelling faster than light, then it would have meant, not that it was a supernatural occurrence, but that the laws which state that nothing can travel faster than light were wrong. However, it seems that the laws still stand and it was the observations that were wrong.

No such problems existed for the world of the Gospel writers. Turning water into wine or walking on water is not possible for most people. They lack the power to do it. Jesus showed his remarkable power in that he could perform such things. It is not a challenge to the understanding of the way the world is constructed or functions; it is simply a mark of the authority over the physical world that this man has. The world of that time had no sense of scientific laws.

We cannot share their perspective. Nor can we challenge their observation. We have to accept their accounts for we have no other and see where it leads our faith and knowledge of Jesus.

Feeding the five thousand

If it is difficult to see the reason for turning water into wine then the feeding of the five thousand seems much more comprehensible. It serves a particular need of a large group of people and it does link with a message of Jesus about feeding the innermost needs of each person. Relatively unusually for John, we have a fairly vague description of how long it was from one event to another. However, it is placed near the time of the Passover. John also explains that this is a Jewish festival, for the benefit of his non-Jewish audience. Why are we given this piece of information? Are we meant to see some significance in the Passover reflected in the miracle? It is very tempting to see this as symbolic and an intended link. But if this is so, surely, we need more explanation. If the writer is having to tell us that the Passover is a Jewish festival, should he not also be telling us what happens at it and how there are parallels between the festival and the miracle? The link is certainly not obvious. It seems to be one of those pieces of detail John puts in because he has it.

This miracle is one of those relatively few events described in all four Gospels. Once again, there are significant similarities but also differences. Both the synoptic account and John's have Jesus going away with his disciples; in Mark, it is to a lonely place, in John, it is up a hill.

John gives no indication that any teaching went on. Jesus is thinking about the food as he sees the crowd approaching. Mark, on the other hand, gives the picture of a daylong teaching. In Mark, it is the disciples who first raise the question of how the crowd is to be fed, but in John, it is Jesus who seems to have a plan in mind all along and asks Phillip what is to be done. The 'testing' was presumably drawing attention to the apparently intractable problem rather than trying to find out if his disciples knew what miracle was required at this point.

All the Gospels agree that it would have taken 200 denarii to buy the bread for the crowd. But it is John only that has the details that it is Andrew who brings the boy to Jesus with the five barley loaves and two fish. In the Synoptics, we are simply told that this is the food they have available. The next point is present in all the Gospels; that Jesus tells the disciples to make the people sit down (although a different word is used in Mark to John). John gives the fascinating little detail that there was plenty of grass. The Synoptics tells us that they were lying on the grass, and Mark adds the adjective green. In all the versions, Jesus gives thanks or says a blessing and then distributes the food. All record that the people were satisfied with the meal and that the fragments were collected filling twelve baskets.

Surely this is the same story told from a slightly different source. Much of the story is clearly identical in fact and feature, but there are some details that vary. John has not copied this from any of the three Synoptic Gospels; this is a clear neat incident in the life of Jesus remembered and recorded in his tradition. As is often the case, John tells us of how people reacted to the miracle—not just the amazement but the response of wanting to make him a king. Not for the first time, John points out that the immediate response of most people is not what Jesus wanted.

It is an interesting detail that shortly further on in the Gospel, when referring back to the incident it is described as 'where the people had eaten the bread over which the Lord had given thanks' (John 6:23). This phrase is not consistently recorded in all texts and so may not be part of the original, but at least some early proponents of the Gospel saw the crucial element of the event was Jesus blessing the food. Not the perspective that comes immediately to us.

Following on from the feeding of the five thousand is the iconic miracle of walking on water. When you consider how little is common to this Gospel and the Synoptics, it is particularly remarkable that this strange incident immediately follows the feeding of the five thousand in Mark, Matthew and John.

In John, one is left wondering why the disciples have got into a boat leaving Jesus behind. The destination, Capernaum, however, is stated. Mark and Matthew explain in more detail what is going on. Jesus is going to dismiss the crowd and then going to pray alone. All three accounts tell us that the sea had got rough, but only Mark and Matthew suggest that the boat was in difficulty because of it.

What then follows is one of the most bizarre and, for us, difficult passages in the Gospels. This is the paradigm of all miracles, walking on water. It seems the most ridiculous, the most unworthy of parables. It sounds like a gimmick. One can understand how the mentally ill, possessed by demons, can be cured by the power of Jesus. One can understand how his compassion moves the power to make the blind see, the deaf hear, the lame walk, even the bereaved reunited with their loved ones, but taking a stroll on a lake! Yet this story is in the Gospels and seems to be a long-remembered incident.

What does seem sensible is the response of the disciples. They are frightened, and in Mark and Matthew it is explained that they thought it was a ghost or apparition. That seems an understandable conclusion. John's account is briefer than Mark's, but it contains most of the essential details in slightly different words. This is another excellent example of a story from the tradition of events in Jesus' life which are recorded by more than one witness. Matthew's account is clearly using the same words as Mark's with just a few alterations. Matthew, of course, then goes on to describe Peter's attempt to walk on water. John is not using a source in the way that Matthew is. He could, of course, have read the account and just put it in his own words but for one who generally gives more details this is unusually brief. It is more likely that he has his own source for the event.

The fascinating extra detail that John inserts is one that is characteristic of the Gospel. It records how people reacted. John explains how the crowd had seen that Jesus had not boarded the boat, the single boat that had left and yet there he was on the other side. "'Rabbi,' they said, 'when did you come here?'" (John 6:26)

The man born blind

The story of the man born blind is a miracle story told in great detail and at some length. A great deal is made of the event. This is a story that is elegantly and clearly told. The conversations that are evoked are presented in a neat and orderly fashion. John takes some time and space to develop the story as the man himself moves from someone who simply reports the facts, through one who asserts that Jesus must be from God to perform such a wonderful act, to the conclusion where he is able to proclaim his faith in Jesus. This man's journey is the one which John wants all his readers to experience; to move from their knowledge about Jesus to faith in him.

The dilemma of why someone should be born blind is presented with the assumption that it is punishment for someone. Jesus repudiates that. He underlines the necessity of doing good while he can. But this episode is being recounted not to go into the question of suffering. It is about sight, and we are presented again with the great acclamation, "I am the light of the world" (John 9:1–5).

There is a detailed description of the precise actions of Jesus in accomplishing the healing with the creation of a paste which is spread on the man's eyes. There is an explanation of the name of the pool, which is ironic, it means 'sent', and then the man regains his sight (John 9:6–7).

What follows is a very realistic and believable account of the response of the neighbourhood. It is an entirely natural response to explain away the apparent miracle by suggesting that there is a confusion of identity. Some people doubt that it is the same person. One can imagine exactly the same response today. Did it really happen? We are told how the man describes the miracle again in detail and attests its truth.

We then learn that the miracle was performed on a Sabbath and that this causes concern to the Pharisees (John 9:13–14). I suppose they are trying to consider whether this is 'black magic' or not and use the abuse of the Sabbath as corroboration for this. The man's testimony before them is factual, and his assessment is surely a contradiction of their views and an opinion that Jesus is a good man of God, someone of significance. This is not meant to say that he is prophesying.

The involvement of the parents is interesting and their response very understandable; they do not want to get involved. It is a potentially dangerous situation and they prefer to be left out of it (John 9:18–23).

In a typical story telling fashion the man gives three accounts of his healing and three statements on his assessment of Jesus. He is summoned again before the Pharisees for a further grilling (John 9:24). What is described is a more heated and bad-tempered argument. It ends with him asserting strongly that Jesus must come from God. In so doing this man is acknowledging the authority that has been discussed so much in the preceding passages. Indeed, again there is the conflicting view of the Jewish authorities asserting that they are disciples of Moses, true to the law and confident that God spoke to Moses, "But as for this fellow we do not know where he comes from." (John 9:29)

The story reaches its climax as Jesus meets the man again. The question is put, "Have you faith in the Son of Man?" (It is interesting to note that some texts put 'Son of God'; the significance of these words was soon confused). There is no greater dramatic irony than Jesus' statement, "You have seen him" (John 9:37). The evangelist is now moving to one of his great themes; the importance of seeing Jesus with the eyes of faith. It contrasts the man's gaining of physical sight with this moment when he gains spiritual sight.

At the end, there is a short dialogue with Jesus emphasising this point by the somewhat riddle-like expression, 'giving sight to the sightless and making blind those who see' (John 9:39). The final point is something extra. The Pharisees are not only unable to see Jesus for who he is but because they claim to know better, they are guilty. Their inability to see is not just a lack of faith but an active opposition to Jesus. This is the Gospel at its very best, with smooth descriptive writing and a cleverly conveyed crucial message of the need to see that Jesus is the Christ, the Son of God so that you may faith.

The pool at Bethesda

The healing of the man at the pool is in many ways more like the miracles recorded in the Synoptics. It is relatively brief for this Gospel. The main point that seems to emerge from it is that Jesus was healing on a Sabbath and the opposition this drew; something that is highlighted by the Synoptics.

Uncharacteristically, it begins with a vague reference to when it happened, 'a Jewish festival' (John 5:10), but then in typical fashion it gives a very detailed explanation as to where the place was with its five colonnades. Attempts to see a symbolic significance in the number of the colonnades seem to me an absurd example of the extent to which some are determined to discredit the authenticity of the Gospel.

What the story does contain are some enigmatic words of Jesus suggesting, as is so often revealed in John, Jesus' knowledge of the individual. His opening challenge is, "Do you want to recover?" (John 5:6). The man's response is fascinatingly illusive. He does not answer the question but gives an excuse as to why he has not been healed. Chronic illness is a terrible and great burden for many, but there are those for whom it simply becomes a way of life. We do not know much about this man, but perhaps for him release from any responsibilities, the need to work, the existence from charity was a pattern of living in which he was entrapped.

Jesus empowers this man. He tells him to pick up his bed and walk. He is empowered to take charge of his own destiny and control his own life. Then at the end of the story is the most intriguing detail of all. Jesus encounters the man again and says, "Now that you are well again, leave your sinful ways, or you may suffer something worse." (John 4:14). What is that all about? We simply do not know, but yet again it seems Jesus knows this person completely.

Raising of Lazarus

The last of the specific miracles is again a long passage with detail and a highly significant conversation on the nature and significance of Jesus. It begins clearly enough by introducing the character of Lazarus who has not previously been mentioned. It explains his relationship to Mary and Martha and then rather curiously explains that Mary is the person who anointed Jesus. This seems to be a curious statement in that the episode where this happens has not yet been described but is placed later in the Gospel.

This could be an example of the alterations made to this Gospel as claimed by some authorities. However, this example of a lack of consistency demonstrates some points about this Gospel which make it different from contemporary books. There is no revision or proofreading. Things are not always expressed in the most logical and systematic way. It might be thought that the recipients of the Gospel are meant to know this story already but then they are likely to know a lot else already, so why pick on this particular detail to circumvent the normal chronological way of describing events?

It is apparent that Jesus knew Lazarus and his sisters well for he 'loved them' (John 11:5). John creates the image that Jesus knew what was going to happen. John makes it clear that Jesus knew that Lazarus was dying and that he intended to perform the miracle of raising him from the dead. Is that what is intended? It seems a rather cruel thing to put Mary and Martha through.

The conversation with the disciples when he decides to go makes perfect sense. They warn him of the danger of going back to the place where people tried to stone him. The answer is enigmatic, "Are there not twelve hours of daylight? Anyone can walk in daytime without stumbling because he sees the light of this world. But if he walks after nightfall, he stumbles because the light fails him" (John 11: 9–10). This response is far from clear. Is Jesus simply saying that there is only limited time to do things I need to do and therefore I need to take the risk? Or is it that we have here a saying of Jesus from a different context that has become introduced into this account? If we are meant to understand the light to be Jesus, such an iconic theme of the Gospel, then it does not seem relevant to Jesus himself making a decision about going back into Judea: he has the light all the time because he is the light of the world.

Thomas presumably thinks that this is a very dangerous place to go, and with a courage that seems to have been lacking later commits himself to go with Jesus even though it means dying with him (John 11:16).

We are told the details of how Martha first meets Jesus whilst Mary stays at home, and then subsequently she is called and joins the discussion. Mary staying at home contrasts with the story in Luke where it is Martha who stays in the kitchen and Mary who sits listening to Jesus.

Does Martha's assertion in the rising of Lazarus at the 'last day' correspond to contemporary Jewish belief? Whilst some Jews did believe in the resurrection was it as an apocalyptic event?

Jesus' reply with its great assertion is very clear, not repetitive, and in a few words presents the essential crux of the Christian Gospel. In contrast to the passages about Jesus as a shepherd, there is a neat discipline with words and a succinct clarity. There is no Amen but the powerful assertion, "I am the resurrection and the life" (John 11:25). Martha responds with the words that are the essential theme of the Gospel, the belief that Jesus is the Messiah, the Son of God.

As when John describes the discovery of Jesus' resurrection, we are given a very detailed account of how and when different people were involved in the unfolding events. The way Mary's friends are described following her out of the house sounds simply like a remembered element of the drama. Few people can have not been struck by the brief but powerful description contained in the words, 'Jesus wept.' This is not an allegory for a piece of theology; this is a dramatic image in a profoundly moving and significant part of John's testimony.

However, there does seem to be a seriously conflicting image of Jesus' reaction and behaviour. On the one hand, he has deliberately delayed coming to Bethany and spoken of God's glory coming. He has said that he will wake Lazarus. He has challenged Martha to believe in him as the source of life. Yet he is distressed at Lazarus' death.

Perhaps Jesus wept because you cannot quantify grief. We do not respond to tragedy, suffering and loss in way that is proportional to the size of the misfortune. We do not feel a slight degree of sadness over the loss of life where twenty or thirty people are killed in some disaster because compared to the loss of life in the Black Death of the middle ages or the 1918 flu epidemic it is a minor event. Grief is simply not like that. Nor do we fail to suffer at the loss of someone we love, someone close to us, because our Christian faith assures us of the glory of the resurrection. It is not an indication of our lack of faith that we grieve. In Jesus, we see this truth demonstrated. Jesus, with the certainty of divine knowledge and the power of God at his command, still feels the loss of someone he has loved. Those tears are a great gift to everyone as they face sadness and tragedy in their own lives.

When I read the second half of verse 42 in which Jesus goes beyond the simple sentence of thanking God for hearing him to explain why he said it, I am very inclined to believe that this is commentary from the evangelist. The explanation is John's opinion as to why Jesus had said these words, for he fears it sounds as though Jesus was not sure of being heard. For me the comment is unnecessary and I suppose I find myself preferring to ascribe it to John than Jesus.

It is of some importance that John describes how Lazarus emerges bound in the cloths with an almost comic image

(John 11:44). It contrasts with the description of how, when Jesus rises from the dead, the disciple entering the tomb notes in particular that the grave clothes are neatly folded in the tomb.

The extreme nature of this miracle jars with modern thinking and beliefs. In the Synoptic Gospels, we have the raising of Jairus' daughter. The fact that Jesus was on the scene so soon after her death softens the impact of the supernatural, and indeed it should be noted that Jesus says she has not died. Conventional thinking is not to take Jesus literally, but that is one possibility. The story in Luke of the raising of the son of the widow of Nain is a brief story, and as such the sceptical can dismiss it as an exaggerated minor event. Such an approach is inappropriate here. This story is a major part of the Gospel and is told in great detail. The burial is several days old. Whilst the diagnosis of death can be difficult and mistakes are not unknown, the intention of the story is quite clear—to make it clear that Jesus has the power to reverse even death itself.

However, the message about Jesus imbedded in it, that he is the resurrection and the life, refers to something else. There is surely no intention to convey the idea that believers are all going to be prevented from going into the tomb and decaying. Here is a clear example of a sign, the much-cherished concept of so many commentators. This is a dramatic event to which is attached the understanding of the transforming power of faith. The concept of the Gospel as a book of signs would work well if all of them had such a clear form.

At the end of the narrative, John yet again tells us how people were affected by what they had seen and how many put their faith in him. He also explains how some people went and told the Pharisees (John 10:45–46). In this Gospel, this particular miracle becomes a pivotal event. There follows an account of how the chief priests and the High Priest in particular decide to put Jesus to death. Jesus goes into hiding, and there is uncertainty as to whether he will attend the Passover.

Jesus does indeed attend, and there is the triumphal Palm waving entry into Jerusalem. The reaction to the raising of Lazarus is given as the reason why so many people came out to see him. John Robinson suggests that Jesus remains largely in hiding and that is why the priests need Judas. He is to help locate Jesus in a situation where he will not be surrounded by crowds.

This great miracle has some very significant and special features. There are the apparently contradictory reactions by Jesus to Lazarus' fatal illness, delaying his departure, asserting his power to raise the dead and weeping over the tomb. There are his enigmatic words about daylight, and then there is the central powerful theme of Jesus giving life represented by the restoration of life to his friend.

Some of the miracles in John are linked to theological teaching and so, of course, provide the basis for the idea of a book of signs. The feeding of the five thousand, the healing of the man born blind and above all, the raising of Lazarus reveal essential parts of the Christian Gospel. However, the healing at the pool of Bethesda and the healing of the officer's son do not carry such clear messages. The turning of water into wine and walking on the water are more perplexing than revealing. In so many ways, John's Gospel fails to be consistent but contains some of the greatest Christian writing.

Chapter 8
Some Features of John

Reaction of Disciples

I suggest one very distinctive feature of John's Gospel is that in addition to telling us the words Jesus used, John also includes the reaction of the disciples to what he was saying and doing. It has a very definite ring of authenticity about it. This is a disciple remembering 'how I felt'. One such instance is John's description of the clearing of the temple. He tells us, 'His disciples recalled the words of Scripture, "Zeal for thy house will destroy me"' (John 2:17), a quotation from Psalm 69:9. John has described a scene of extreme disruption in the temple with an attack on the well-established trading practices associated with it; practices that were probably a major part of the economy of the temple and to some extent Jerusalem. It is easy to understand that this was a potentially dangerous and provocative act. The comment is couched cleverly as a scriptural reference, but the point is very clear. The disciples feared that Jesus was putting his life in danger and thereby possibly themselves as well.

Another example is in the story of the woman at the well in the Samaritan village. The conversation with the woman occurs whilst the disciples have gone off to find food. After a lot of detail of the conversation, the narrative describes the moment when the disciples return. John describes their reaction. They are astonished to find him talking to this woman. That they should find this peculiar is not under the circumstances surprising, but the writer goes on to tell us the very personal detail of how they felt unable to either admonish the woman or ask Jesus what he is about. One can feel the awkwardness of the disciples. To me, it has a definite quality of a testimony from someone who was there. We even learn how they got themselves out of their embarrassment; they tried to persuade Jesus to come and eat. Apparently, Jesus was in no hurry. He was concerned to bring this woman to an understanding of the kingdom of God.

This brief part of the story is, for me, a powerful testimony of the historical accuracy of this account. This a human encounter with all the complexities of people's prejudices, embarrassment, and attempts to say things to manoeuvre the situation, that we all know and experience. This is recorded because it is a vivid memory and shows Jesus' priority in his concern for this woman's future.

'The Jews'

In John's Gospel, one group of people are identified repeatedly as 'the Jews.' All the Gospels give a significant prominence to the conflict that arose between Jesus and those who were in a position of religious authority. Indeed, they stress that it was the senior clerics of Jerusalem who arranged for his arrest, brought him before Pilate and urged his crucifixion. The Synoptic Gospels describe conflict throughout Jesus' ministry before the final visit to Jerusalem as being with Pharisees, Sadducees and Scribes. One of the features of John's Gospel is that in the narrative of Jesus' ministry before the final days, the opposition is described simply as, 'the Jews'. What did John mean? Who are the Jews?

It cannot be seriously entertained that the writer was unaware that Jesus and his disciples were Jews. Why then is the broad expression used? When the Synoptic Gospels specify that Jesus is challenged by Pharisees, lawyers, doctors of the law, elders; these are clearly groups of people of which Jesus and his disciples were not part.

I do not believe that we have a definite explanation. The term suggests that the book was written for people who did not consider themselves to be Jews. One possible explanation that has been put forward is that, by the time the book was written, there was already intense opposition from Jewish communities and synagogues to the Christians. Thus the Jews were identified as 'the enemy' and so are portrayed as those opposed to Jesus during his ministry. However, if the book is earlier in construction than many suppose then this is no longer a working hypothesis. Even if the Gospel was written after the Jewish opposition had become established, it would represent a rather crude approach, particularly as the Synoptics have pointed the blame at groups like the Pharisees and the lawyers. The problem that Jesus and his disciples were clearly Jewish remains.

One possible interpretation is that it means people from Judea. When describing Jesus visiting Galilee after the journey through Samaria, the Gospel does refer to the people as Galileans (John 4:45). When a deputation is sent out from

Jerusalem, and therefore from within Judea, to question John the Baptist about his ministry, these people are referred to as Jews (John 1:19).

However, the conversations described in Chapter 6 after Jesus has walked on the sea of Galilee are between Jesus and the Jews. The term is used a couple of times, and yet the whole section is sandwiched between a definite statement that they had gone to Capernaum and a statement at the end that these things were spoken in the synagogue at Capernaum, which is clearly in Galilee. It does not seem that interpreting 'Jews' as people from Judea works as a consistent explanation.

My suggestion is that it is meant to be a vague description. Nearly everyone around was Jewish and perhaps one should simply substitute the word 'people' for it. In the conversation with the woman by the well there is the rather surprising remark that, "It is from the Jews that salvation comes" (John 4:22). This runs against any general impression that Jews were the problem. Perhaps John was less inclined to pin the blame for the persecution of Jesus on any particular group, but ironically history has taken his word to do just that.

Puzzles and questions

John's Gospel contains some very neat and elegant pieces of writing. The prologue is one, the description of the clearing of the temple is recounted with dramatic simplicity, and the brief and bleak words of 13:30 when Judas having been identified as the betrayer leaves the Last Supper: 'And it was night,' are examples of genius. On the other hand, there are parts of the Gospel that seem confusing. It is easy to understand why many have suggested that the Gospel has been 'cut and pasted' and that perhaps more than once. Here are some examples.

In Chapter 3:22–24 there is some surprising information. Mark and Matthew are quite clear that Jesus did not start his ministry until John was arrested. 'After John had been arrested, Jesus came into Galilee proclaiming the Gospel of God' (Mark 1:14 and Matthew 4:12–17). Luke is not clear on this. However, they certainly do not associate Jesus' ministry with baptism by water which John's Gospel does. In absolute contradiction to the Synoptics, John tells us, 'Jesus went into Judea with his disciples, stayed there with them and baptised. John too was baptising…' (John 3:22–23) In typical Johannine fashion, we are given some details about places and with the prosaic explanation that this is because there was plenty of water in this place.

What is particularly curious is that the statement that Jesus was baptising is contradicted in 4:2. It is made as a point of clarification that it was the disciples not Jesus who was baptising. Why does John need to make this alteration? If it was his disciples that were baptising, then why not make it clear the first time the matter is raised (John 4:22)? Why was this not sorted out before publication? Is this an example of the way the Gospel is written? The writing materials are so precious and if the writer is using a scroll, then rather than start again, the misunderstanding is corrected later. One can imagine someone pointing out that it reads as though Jesus was baptising and the writer then wishing to clarify it.

On the other hand, is this a later addition in an attempt to deny something that was originally stated in the Gospel? Later thinking wanted to stress that Jesus' baptism was in the Spirit not water. If this is the case, it is perhaps surprising that the alteration was not made to the first reference. It remains something of mystery and a rather awkward glitch in the Gospel.

It is in any case an example of the Gospel saying something quite different to the synoptic tradition with detail that serves no significant theological purpose. This is not a late Gospel putting some particular spin on the message. It is rather the rough and at times inconvenient details of how things actually happened.

The statement about baptism is followed by the account of the woman by the well. The opening of the next episode begins with an enigmatic statement. Jesus continues his journey to Galilee, the destination described before the interlude in Samaria. However, we are then told, 'Jesus himself declared that a prophet is without honour in his own country' (John 4:44). This comment does not seem to make sense. What it seems to be is an explanation of why Jesus should not go to the place to which he is going. Biblical scholars have tended to interpret this statement as meaning that Jesus was referring to Jerusalem and then come up with an explanation of why Jesus should refer to that city as his own country— 'Jerusalem is the home of every true prophet.'

The Synoptic Gospels tell of Jesus making this self-same statement about Nazareth. One of the most basic facts about Jesus is that he was known as Jesus of Nazareth. It seems odd that John should suddenly anticipate that we all understand that Jesus saw himself as, in some sort of spiritual sense, belonging to Jerusalem. This is the writer who has so helpfully just explained that Jews and Samaritans would not share the same drinking vessels.

This statement surely does refer to Galilee. There is an unexplained anomaly in that it makes no sense to put it as a reason for him going to Galilee, and it seems to be contradicted by the next few sentences which describe his welcome there. However one chooses to look at it, this is an awkward point in the narrative. My view is that Jesus is speaking about Galilee and the writer is using the words Jesus spoke about his ministry in Nazareth and which are recorded in the Synoptic Gospels with the account of his visit there.

The opening verse of chapter 6 contains a slightly awkward transition. The preceding passage has been about Jesus in Jerusalem and what he has said there. Then the Gospel says, 'Sometime later Jesus withdrew to the farther shore of the Sea of Galilee' (John 6:1). To have moved from Jerusalem to Galilee is quite a significant change in location. It is not a major problem but raises the question whether this is a story which originally followed an event much closer to the Sea of Galilee.

Another curious passage is the dialogue where John tells us that, 'Turning to the Jews who had believed him, Jesus said, "If you dwell within the revelation I have brought, you are indeed my disciples; you shall know the truth, and the truth will set you free"' (John 8:30). However, within a few sentences of dialogue, Jesus is then saying to these people, "but you are bent on killing me" (John 8:37), and "Your father is the devil" (John 8:44). One cannot but wish there was something more of an explanation as to how a group of people who are introduced as doing the very thing the Gospel writer is urging on us all, believing in Jesus, are so rapidly vehemently attacked by Jesus.

These awkward passages provide ammunition for those who wish to lower the status of John's Gospel, but there are problem passages in all the Gospels. Perhaps they should be seen as evidence of the relatively unsophisticated construction of the book at an early stage. The passion of the writer has not always translated into perfect composition. The very different way in which such a book would have been produced and reproduced from a book today must also be factor in understanding why such difficulties arise.

Although it is not a difficulty in the sense we have been considering, this seems a suitable point to mention the problematic short story of the woman brought to Jesus for judgement. The traditional formulation of the Gospel, the one found in the 1611 King James version, has the story of the woman taken in adultery at the start of Chapter 8. Modern translations point out that it is missing from the most ancient texts and is found in other places including within Luke's Gospel. It is a dramatic and powerful story but the vocabulary and style are different from all else in the Gospel. It seems likely that it was written by someone completely different.

Other than that Jesus is in Jerusalem, the story does not really fit into the narrative of John at this moment. In many ways, the manner of the encounter and what Jesus says are more suggestive of the synoptic tradition. What is a striking dramatic detail is the way Jesus writes in the ground. That is perhaps the sort of memorable and distinctive detail that John seems to use, as is also the way the crowd are described dispersing, the eldest first. However, the balance of opinion would suggest that it is not really part of John's original Gospel.

It is not difficult to imagine how this passage came to be 'orphaned'. The situation is highly controversial. Here is a woman caught in the very act of sexual intercourse with someone who is not her husband, and Jesus does not condemn her. This is not a message that would be comfortable for the leaders of the church trying to encourage people to live upright and holy lives. I do not doubt that it is an entirely genuine historical event, just one that was a bit too radical for most people. Why it came to be incorporated into this Gospel is a mystery, one of many that surround the book. It is an incident in the temple and, of course, the Synoptics have Jesus visiting Jerusalem only once in his ministry. It more conveniently, therefore, sits in John's narrative so that it does not become another event in the final days.

Furthermore, the final message that Jesus does not condemn but rather requires a change in people fits well with the general themes of John's Gospel. The great words of 3:16 are followed by, "It was not to judge (or condemn) the world that God sent his Son into the world, but through him the world might be saved." This is the real significance of what Jesus says to the woman. He does not say that she has not done wrong. Indeed, he tells her not to sin again. What he is saying is that the woman is not condemned by her wrongdoing. Jesus came to release people from sin not punish them; as Charles Wesley puts it in his great hymn, And can it be, *no condemnation now I dread.*

Seeing

John's Gospel contains some key themes and words. One of the most important is 'seeing'. The word appears many times from the beginning to the end. John plays on the varied meaning of seeing from the optical phenomenon to perception and understanding. He is aware that whilst many people were able to cast their eyes on Jesus as he walked around Judea and Galilee, many failed to see in him the Christ. He is writing for a large audience who had no chance of observing the events described in the Gospel but who, he hopes, will see in Jesus the source of eternal life. The theme is apparent as part of the great prologue where John proclaims that we saw his glory. At the climax of the story of Chapter 20, which is possibly the original ending of the book, John has Jesus declaring to Thomas, "Happy are they who never saw me and yet have found faith" (John 20:29).

It is intriguing that one of the first conversations we are given in John's Gospel is the encounter with Nathaniel. I have referred to it earlier when discussing the way Jesus has insight into other people's personality. However, this encounter also brings out the fundamental theme of seeing in this curious conversation. There is surely a comical aspect to this episode. We cannot judge how humorously this was intended, but I venture to suggest that John has included it with a sense of amusement as much as anything else.

Nathaniel makes a derogatory remark about Nazareth. Philip's response is an invitation to, "Come and see." Nathaniel is given the opportunity to see for himself the person in question and to make his own judgement. Jesus greets Nathaniel and does so demonstrating one of the characteristics that John emphasises about him, his knowledge of his personality. Here is a man of integrity, true to his heritage, says Jesus. Nathaniel does not respond with any false modesty; there is no attempt to contradict Jesus.

"How do you come to know me?" asks Nathaniel (John 1:48). Jesus replies by saying that he has seen him under the fig tree.

Many have made much of the fig tree suggesting that it is a reference to the iconic image of the Jewish person sitting under his own fig tree. I suggest that the emphasis is on the seeing rather than the tree. Jesus saw Nathaniel.

Nathaniel's response is over the top and surely Jesus is somewhat amused by it. Nathaniel has swung from scepticism about somebody from Nazareth to a belief that he has met the 'Son of God, the king of Israel' (John 1:49). It is a somewhat absurd swing in opinion and perhaps Jesus is amused by it. He thinks that an odd ground for faith and assures Nathaniel that, 'You ain't seen nothing yet!' But then Jesus comes out with a pronouncement which is given the 'Amen, amen' introduction that assures Nathaniel that he will see heaven's glory. Nathaniel is going to see something truly special. To Nathaniel will come the sight of the glory of God with angels ascending and descending. As sublime as it gets.

We have already considered the detailed story of the curing of the man born blind which is, of course, all about seeing. The man himself moves from the restoration of his physical sight to an understanding of the goodness of Jesus as he argues with the Jewish authorities and then to his confrontation with Jesus where he declares his faith. This is in response to the powerfully dramatic irony of the words of Jesus, "You have seen him" (John 9:37). The coda to the story in which Jesus speaks of the blindness of the Pharisees emphasises the theme of the crucial need to see Jesus as the Christ and have faith in him.

There is a curiously enigmatic scene in which some Greeks come to Philip and say, "Sir, we should like to see

Jesus" (John 12:21). It is enigmatic because there is no account of whether they did see Jesus. Jesus' comments are about his crucifixion. This passage is concluded by John quoting from Isaiah, 'He has blinded their eyes and dulled their minds, lest they should see with their eyes, and perceive with their minds, and turn to me to heal them' (John 12:40, a reference to Isaiah 6:10).

As part of the farewell discourse, Jesus' words are quoted, "A little while and you see me no more; again a little while, and you will see me" (John 16:16). The balanced cryptic nature of this remark sounds like a direct quote from Jesus. It foretells of their grief at the crucifixion and their joy at the resurrection but in terms of what they will see.

The account of the resurrection experience of the beloved disciple, whom I believe to be John, and the source of the Gospel, is described closely around what is seen; how he peers into the tomb and what he sees, how Peter enters and sees the details of the grave clothes, and then the climax is declared in the simple words, 'and he saw and believed.' This is the centre of faith for John: see in the events and person of Jesus the source of everlasting life and have faith.

Everlasting Life

For John the gift that God makes available through Jesus is life, everlasting life. In the Synoptic Gospels, the message of the good news is about the coming of the kingdom, the kingdom of God. Thus in Mark's Gospel as Jesus begins his ministry, he proclaims the message, "The time has come; the kingdom of God is upon you" (Mark 1:15). The word 'kingdom' is used 20 times in Mark, 55 times in Matthew and

46 times in Luke, but only 5 times in John. The Synoptics see the kingdom as the new order that Jesus is bringing about. John is clearly much more reticent to use the word.

One instance is when Jesus is talking to Nicodemus. He tells Nicodemus that unless someone is born again, "he cannot see the kingdom of God" (John 3:3), and shortly afterwards in the same theme, "no one can enter the kingdom of God without being born from water and spirit" (John 3:5). Why this one piece of dialogue uses this form of words when in every other instance the kingdom is not an expression used, is a mystery.

The other occurrence of the word 'kingdom' is exceptional in that it is about the very use of the word. In Jesus' trial before Pilate, Pilate challenges him with the question, "Are you the king of the Jews?" Jesus replies, "My kingdom does not belong to this world." He goes on to say that if his kingdom was, then his servants would be fighting but rather his kingdom is not from here (John 18:33–37).

What is at stake here is the role of Jesus. Jesus is very careful to avoid attaching the wrong label to his position. Other people may have suggested he is a king but not in the sense which threatens the rule of Rome; this is not a political challenge. "King is your word," Jesus tells Pilate.

Why has John focused on the expression life rather than kingdom? Is it fear that Roman authority will see Christianity as a threat? Is it John who has made the change or is it rather the Synoptics who have emphasised a usage? When the kingdom of the Jews is collapsing, Jerusalem destroyed, is it perhaps important to explain that there is a new kingdom, the kingdom of God?

The theme of everlasting life is part of the words which are perhaps the most famous of all within the Gospel, John 3:16, "God so loved the world that he gave his only Son, that everyone who has faith in him may not die but have eternal life." The final words of the first ending of the Gospel (John 20:31) make it clear that life is the promise of the Gospel message.

The kingdom that is spoken of in the Synoptics is sometimes the kingdom of God and sometimes the kingdom of heaven. Just as the evangelists struggle to find the right words to describe the status of Jesus so also, they use different words to describe the benefits of faith. For John it is clear that the transforming power of the Gospel makes the most supreme difference, as great as life and death. Which words did Jesus use? Presumably he used both, and different writers have focused on one rather than the other.

Chapter 9
Special Passages in John

Prologue

In places, John's Gospel contains some very great writing and its opening is as famous as it is grand and powerful. This is writing of the very highest quality. Indeed, the prologue can be considered some of the greatest writing in world literature. There is surely no greater opening to a book.

John's Gospel is, I contend, centred on the question of the nature of Jesus. Who is he and what is his relationship to God? The book starts confronting this issue head on. To do this, he introduces an entirely unique concept and expression, the Word. In so doing, John emphasises that Jesus' position is quite unique, quite unlike anything else we might imagine or experience. The phrases have a circular structure which emphasises the unity between the Word and God. Thus 'When all things began the Word already was and dwelt with God' is followed by, 'The word was with God at the beginning.' This is repetition but not of a superfluous nature. The passage has a robust authority because of it.

It also introduces two of the major themes of the book, life and light. Seeing Jesus as the source of life is the core message of the evangelist. Identifying Jesus as light and the contrast between light and darkness are a recurring way of expressing the struggle to accept Jesus; the personal struggle and the conflict that surrounded him. From Philip's challenge to Nathaniel to come and see, the healing of the man born blind and through to the evangelist's witness that he 'saw and believed' at the empty tomb, seeing and light are two of the most important words for this author.

Verse 5 is rendered in the NEB as, 'The light shines on in the dark and the darkness has never mastered it.' As I understand it, the word translated 'mastered' can be translated in two ways. It can mean 'understood' or 'comprehended' as the AV familiarly puts it. It can also mean to overcome or overpower. The NEB's use of 'master' cleverly encompasses both meanings. I suggest that the genius writer of the Gospel deliberately used a word with an ambiguous meaning, for both are truths about the Gospel message. Those opposed to Jesus have not understood him nor have they had the power to destroy the Gospel.

The use of the concept of 'The Word,' suggests links to Greek philosophy, but this is not the general style of the book. There are those who have gone on to see other themes in the book as references to other philosophies. But the Gospel is mostly very straightforward. It explains details and tries to avoid obscurity. The reference to the Logos at the beginning is as plainly stated as possible. The use of this special term is the genius of the author in trying to explore what ultimately is a mystery, the nature of the Christ.

The use of a somewhat esoteric-sounding Greek word has encouraged some to suggest that the prologue is an addition to the Gospel, written at a later date and by someone different.

If it is not the beginning then what is? In contrast at the other end of the book there is an epilogue which follows the fairly obvious ending of the Gospel at the end of Chapter 20. There is good reason to think that Chapter 21 is an addition. There is no such parallel at the start. This sounds like a great beginning and the immediate claim to the central message of the book. Jesus is one with God and is God's revelation to mankind.

Morna Hooker in her book *Beginnings*[1] says that the two passages in the prologue about the Baptist, 1: 6–9 and 1:15, are a break from the 'exalted style' of the rest. They are very prosaic and break into the flowing rhythmic description of the Word. Are they an addition to the prologue?

The passage certainly works without these few verses, but I think the contrast is not as clear cut as Hooker would have us believe. John's appearance is a sudden step in the flowing passage, but this may be a deliberate literary feature and almost immediately we find John the Baptist described in terms of witnessing to the light, the concept that has just been introduced.

At first, one might think verse 15, the second mention of the Baptist does seem to be just out of position. The following two verses seem to go back to verse 14. The statement about John's testimony given in verse 15 does break into the otherwise fluent and continuous statement. Furthermore in just a short paragraph later, there is another account of the Baptist's testimony.

The start of the account of the Baptist at verse 19 seems clumsy if verse 15 precedes it immediately. It is not as though verse 15 has become displaced in front of verses 16 to 18. Furthermore, they are different in that verse 15 talks of John's general testimony to Jesus and verse 19 onwards to a specific reply given to a deputation asking who the Baptist was.

Part of the Baptist's testimony described in verse 15 are the words, "before I was born, he already was" (John1:15). An important point made in the prologue is to express the view that Jesus existed before his birth because of his oneness with God. John the Baptist seems to be affirming this point in the statement inserted at verse 15. Hence it belongs in the prologue. There is a logic to the arrangement, and I do not think we should conclude that any part of the first 18 verses of the Gospel have been inserted at a later date.

If the whole book has been written to try and explain the nature and purpose of Christ, then it is appropriate that the writer proceeds to state John the Baptist's contribution. The main content of the conversations described is that Jesus is coming, the Christ. Whereas the other Gospel writers may be keen to tell us of the Baptist's teaching, what John gives us is his reference to Christ.

Following straight on from John's relationship with Jesus is the call of some of the disciples including Nathaniel. Within the relatively short opening part of the book we have had Jesus described as Word, Light, Lamb of God, God's chosen one, the Messiah and the explanation that this is Hebrew for Christ, Son of God and King of Israel, and Jesus' own expression, the Son of Man. There is no shortage of labels or titles. The problem for the apostle, for the emerging church, is to explain what they mean.

Mark starkly commences his Gospel with the use of the title Christ for Jesus and perhaps with the assertion that he is the Son of God. This latter phrase is one of those that are missing from some of the oldest texts. Matthew and Luke explore the question of the nature of Jesus by describing his birth, firstly, in relation to his heritage from David and then by the miracle of the Virgin Birth to indicate his divine nature. John, I suggest, is ready to demonstrate that there are many different labels, but that it is for us to see and believe for ourselves.

The Samaritan Woman

The story of the woman at the well is told at length and in detail. It centres around a conversation. We are given a specific reason why Jesus was travelling in this direction. The location is specified and its relation to the well of Jacob, something that has relevance in the following discussion. Although we are not given a calendar date, we are told the time of day. The few simple words paint a clear picture of Jesus, like any person, tired after a journey sitting down for a rest at the height of the day. The disciples go for food leaving him alone and so the scene is set for the odd situation of a Samaritan woman on her own, and Jesus, the teacher also on his own.

The conversation with the Samaritan woman at the well begins with a request for a drink of water. John explains the peculiarity and anomaly of a Jew asking for water from a Samaritan. It is an important example of John's style. He is writing for people who might not be familiar with Jewish customs and so he needs to explain them. More significantly is the very fact that he thinks important to explain things, to clarify. John is not in the business of writing a book with hidden meanings and coded references. This is a book from which people can learn vital truths plainly stated.

What then follows is again something typical of Jesus as he is described in all the Gospels. He starts a conversation with a cryptic remark, a comment which Jesus knows full well that the woman will not understand—he can give her living water; something that must have sounded as mysterious and incomprehensible as Jesus surely knew full well Nicodemus would not understand being born again. This is how Jesus engages people in important dialogue. From remarks about whether or not he has a bucket, we are in a few moments hearing that God is Spirit and those who worship him must worship in spirit and truth.

It is interesting that Jesus speaks of himself as a source of living water, but this is not transposed into a saying such as 'I am the water of life' which, of course, is a style of description peculiar to John. So Jesus has this conversation where clearly the woman does not appreciate that he is talking of spiritual matters even to the point that she asks for the water of life to avoid the chore of collecting water from the well.

Then Jesus switches the conversation from this somewhat teasing and intriguing introduction by demonstrating how much he knows of her. As John has declared before, Jesus knows people. He knows her to be living with someone she is not married to. The insight transforms the woman's attitude and now begins a discussion on the differences between the Jews and Samaritans. Her comment seems to be a sudden change in direction on her part, but it serves for Jesus to deliver a message about true worship being a matter of spirit and truth.

What is remarkable and unusual is that Jesus clearly states that he is the Messiah, something that elsewhere he avoids and usually tells others not to go about telling others. What is different about this situation? Does the fact that he is in Samaria rather than in a Jewish community mean that the impact and consequences of such an assertion are very different? Of course, the source of this conversation must be the woman's own recollection and account. Perhaps she believed she heard Jesus assert something in a way that had not actually happened.

I have already commented on the way John describes the disciples' reaction and how they try and manage the situation. That John should describe what they were thinking and yet what they did not dare say is, to me, a powerful indication that this account comes directly from someone who was there, the son of Zebedee himself.

Cleansing the temple

John's description of the cleansing of the temple (John 2:14–22) is a great example of his clear narrative style. Many people would be surprised to discover how much of their image of this event derives from John's description rather than the Synoptics. They do little more than reference it.

John's account contains more detail but not at the expense of elaborate description or symbolism. John tells us that in the temple there were dealers in cattle, sheep and pigeons whereas the Synoptics speak only of the birds. Jesus makes a whip out of cords; clearly something necessary to drive this collection of large animals out of the courtyard and describes Jesus driving the animals out. 'He upset the tables of the moneychangers, scattering their coins.' In these few words, John draws a picture of turmoil and dramatic disturbance: the coins spilling on to the ground as he upends the tables and the different animals being herded from the precincts. He does not describe the reactions of the people as these coins are scattered, but one can envisage the chaos as the dealers try to retrieve the coins and no doubt others try to collect them. Does not the whole episode become alive with this neat and briefly described narrative?

In John, Jesus tells the pigeon sellers to take them out. This makes sense. One could not drive out birds; they would be in cages. Jesus could have released them but none of the Gospels suggest that is what he did nor is he trying to take from the dealers their property. He is trying to clear the temple of their activity and make the temple once again a place of prayer rather than a market. John's detail is sensible and credible.

Although this is an event described by the Synoptics, they put it at a different stage in his ministry. For John, it is something right at the beginning, but they put it as part of the final episode in Jerusalem after Jesus has made his triumphal entry and shortly before his arrest.

There can be little doubt that the same incident is being described in the Synoptic Gospels and in John. The Synoptics are constructed in such a way that Jesus goes to Jerusalem during his ministry only once. It makes a neat dramatic account. John has Jesus visiting at least three times during his ministry which is more complicated. Is this not simply an example of where John is telling us how it happened historically whereas the Synoptics have tidied it up to make a neater story?

As mentioned earlier, John Robinson makes the point that if it were something that happened in the last few days before his arrest, why was it not mentioned at Jesus' trial?

The anointing of Jesus

Another example of powerful simple description is the story of the anointing of Jesus (John 12:1–8). It is one of the events that is in the Synoptics. Indeed, it is special in that it is Luke rather than John which seems to have the major differences. In fact, Luke's story is so different in many ways that one wonders if it is in fact a different event. In Luke's account, Jesus is at the house of a Pharisee called Simon and is given a lot of attention by a woman who was known as a prostitute or considered immoral. The story centres around whether Jesus knows this and how he reacts to it. It ends with him forgiving her sins. There is no mention of the anointing for burial and no discussion about the cost. Perhaps the perfume has got added into this story as a misunderstood connection to the story in Mark, Matthew and John.

The versions in Matthew and Mark are closely aligned. They say that the meal was at the house of Simon the leper in Bethany. John agrees that the incident took place in Bethany; not necessarily in the house of Lazarus. The detail is used to clarify the place. However, Martha is serving which does imply that it might well have been their house. Mary is the woman who does the anointing whereas in Mark and Matthew there is no identification at all. The perfume is nard in both Mark's and John's accounts but the alabaster jar is not mentioned in John.

The perfume is poured on the head of Jesus in Matthew and Mark but on the feet in John. Mary uses her hair to wipe them, something which ties in with the version in Luke. John then includes a phrase which is powerful in its imagery, 'the house was filled with the perfume.' Robinson cites this as an example of something remembered by someone who was there. Smell certainly does have great power in memory and one can well imagine that people who were there would be struck by the overwhelming sensation of this expensive and strong perfume so lavishly poured permeating throughout the house. If it is not a true memory, it demonstrates great literary skill in the author.

John agrees with the first two Synoptics on the value of the perfume, 300 denarii. In Mark, it is just some of the company who complain about the waste, in Matthew it is the disciples, but in John this is specified as Judas. There follows an unusual piece of propaganda against Judas. We are told he had no care for the poor but that he was a thief and pilfered out of the shared money of the group for which he had charge. One can well imagine that after the passion a lot of bad things were said about Judas. It is not surprising that such an opinion was rife.

Jesus' response is one of protection for the woman, "Leave her alone." This is expanded in the two Synoptics. There is the assertion that you will always have the poor but not me. John's version is briefer. Both versions then mention his burial, but in Mark and Matthew Jesus says she has anointed his body for burial beforehand whereas in John he says that she should keep it until the day when she prepares his body for burial. The final great assertion of the two Synoptics that this woman's action will be told wherever the Gospel is proclaimed is missing from John. To me, this is highly suggestive of an earlier version of the story whereas for Mark and Matthew this prophecy is quite evidently becoming true.

This story clearly seems to be the same event. As I have said, it is possible that Luke's account is something different.

Yet equally clearly there are a lot of differences in detail. John surely cannot have copied this from the Synoptics. Why would he change all these details? This must be from a separate source. The evidence of the memory of the smell makes a case for John's account being the more reliable historical version. On the other hand it is difficult to know why the Synoptics would not include the identity of the woman if it was the sister of Lazarus. Whatever else, it seems to me that this is strong evidence that John contains early separate sources.

What more is there to say?

We have already noted that the way Jesus speaks in John's Gospel is characteristic of it and quite different for the most part from the Synoptics. This is never more evident than in the section that begins at Chapter 13 and ends at the start of Chapter 18 with Jesus leaving for the garden where he is arrested. It starts with a number of different dialogues and concludes with a monologue or rather a prayer.

It seems highly unlikely that this whole section is an accurate historical account of everything that was uttered on that Thursday evening over supper. This must have been a compilation of things Jesus said. The Gospel tells us that Jesus was aware that the crisis was upon him, (John 13:3), and therefore it is reasonable to presume that this was therefore his last chance to teach and speak to his closest followers. It would not be surprising, therefore, if he did not say some highly significant and important things. Jesus will very likely have delivered some crucial and memorable statements.

However, there is likely to be other material in this passage as well, sayings that were heard at other times.

In addition to this being a record of the last opportunity Jesus had to address his disciples before his arrest, it is also the conclusion of that part of the Gospel which has been exploring the nature of Jesus, his relationship to God and the central theme of having faith in him to give eternal life. There is therefore also a sense in which it is John's last chance to put together his thoughts on the subject before giving us the much more factual account of the arrest, trial and crucifixion of Jesus; a section which is then followed by the distinctively personal accounts of the resurrection.

The narrative begins with an account of Jesus washing his disciples' feet. This is one of those highly significant and powerful images which has greatly influenced Christian thinking throughout the centuries and yet is recorded solely in this Gospel. It is so peculiar and unexpected that it must be historically true. However, why then do the other Gospels not mention it? Was it that this was a concept too far for some of the early Christians? Here is the Christ who is being worshipped and prayed to, being one with the Father, and yet washing the feet of this group of people which include the traitor. This is an example where it seems possible that John has the historical accuracy and the Synoptics have suppressed it.

John's Gospel gives a relatively extended account of Jesus acknowledging the existence of one who is to betray him and identifying him to at least Peter and John. In the Synoptics, Jesus announces that one of the company will betray him. The disciples are shocked and ask, "Is it I?" Only in Matthew is there any further comment about identifying Judas and it is recorded as a conversation between the two with little more than an ironic response from Jesus, "The words are yours" (Matthew 26:25). The way it is described in John, with the signalled revelation of Judas' identity by Jesus giving him some bread, suggests that it was a secret known only to the beloved disciple, John, and presumably Peter. Again the descriptive detail gives it a great sense of authenticity.

This dramatic episode ends with one of the phrases in John that demonstrates the enormous power of the writing. Judas goes out and we are told, 'It was night' (John 13:30); the image of Judas leaving the assembled company around Jesus to go into the dark, away from the light and the fellowship. This is one of the darkest moments in the history of the human race. It was night in every sense. These few simple words of the Gospel writer encapsulate the situation.

Jesus speaks about going away, something that is highly relevant in the context of this occasion. He starts in verse 33 of Chapter 13, and there is dialogue going on to verse 6 of Chapter 14. However, he returns to the same theme in verses 18, 28 and then again in Chapter 16 verse 4. Here there is an apparent contradiction. Jesus says, "None of you asks me 'Where are you going?'" (John 16:5), and yet quite clearly in 14:5 Thomas says, "Lord, we do not know where you are going." It is not the exact question phrased by Jesus, but it is stretching the point to say that the disciples have not questioned what Jesus means by talking about going away.

The subject comes up again a little further on. In verse 19, he talks of how in a little while they will not see him and then they will (John 16:19), and then again in verse 28, "Now I am leaving the world again and going to the Father." Apparently, the disciples greet this as plain speaking unlike what has been said before.

The implication of all this is surely that we have a collection of things said about Jesus going away, and they are collated in a not very systematic piece of editing where the topic keeps recurring between other matters.

Just as there are a number of separated statements about Jesus leaving, there are also statements about the Advocate, the Holy Spirit, intermittently brought into the dialogue (John 14:16–17; 14:26; 15:26; 16:7–11).

Another feature of this long passage is the inclusion of a number of comments about the impending persecution and difficulties of the future church. There is talk of the world hating them (John 15:18–21), and then a much more specific problem, "They will ban you from the synagogue" (John 16:2) and the warning that people will believe it is their religious duty to kill them (John 16:2). Whenever in the Gospels we read prophecies and warnings of the future dangers facing the disciples and the church, it raises the possibility that these are insertions reflecting the experiences of the church contemporary to the time of writing. At the very least, of course, the relevance of such sayings will influence the inclusion of such statements. Are they genuine or teaching from the church leaders to encourage the faithful by putting the words into the mouth of Jesus? Nobody knows. The more specific the warnings, banning from the synagogue, for example, the more likely it seems that it is a detail added after Pentecost and not the exact words of Christ.

What this passage also contains in addition to these matters relating to Jesus' passion and the struggles for the church are some of his more general teachings. In fact, here are some of the great sayings of John's Gospel. There are the great 'I am' sayings of, "I am the vine" (John 15:5), and "I am the way, I am the truth and I am life" (John 14:6). There is a repeated command to love one another. It is given near the beginning of this section (John 13:34), and it comes again following the declaration that Jesus is the vine (John 15:9–17).

There is a story of someone seeing Hamlet for the first time and naively saying that it was a string of quotations put together, not realising how many famous phrases originate from this one play. Likewise, one might feel that this is a collation of some of the most famous texts. "There are many dwelling places in my Father's house" (John 14.2) and "Peace is my parting gift to you" (John 14.27) are two examples of these great utterances.

The treasured and important character of these sayings is not something particular to our generation, and they must have meant as much to the earliest followers of Jesus as they do today. This section has therefore drawn together as a climax this material. The way it repeats and does not follow a particular logical sequence suggests to me that it is a compilation and not a reconstruction of the sequence of things Jesus said on that occasion. Once again, we cannot know which were said on that evening, and how much has been brought together by an author or by the teaching of John.

Then we come to one of the most unusual sections of this and of any of the Gospels, Chapter 17, the 'High Priestly Prayer'. Whereas the previous sayings have been described as a dialogue with the disciples and individuals, named on occasions, asking questions, this section is Jesus addressing God in prayer. At times, however, it seems to include statements about Jesus and his relationship with the disciples rather than a credible prayer of Jesus talking to God. "This is eternal life; to know you the only true God, and Jesus Christ whom you have sent" (REB John 17:3) sounds like a statement from John. It is again the key message of the Gospel, and although Jesus sometimes uses a title such as the Son of Man to speak about himself, it seems difficult to believe that in a prayer he would actually speak of himself as Jesus Christ.

If warnings of persecution would seem important to the early church so even more so would these words of concern, love and encouragement. The idea of Jesus in the course of an evening meal stopping addressing his disciples and praying aloud these words is hard to accept as an historical event. This passage is perhaps the paradigm of the accounts of Jesus' speaking in John that have been a major force in leading so many to consider the whole Gospel as secondary and historically inaccurate.

Where have these words come from? I believe we should consider them to represent a distillation of things said by Jesus to his close friend and confidant, the disciple whom Jesus loved, John.

References

1. Hooker, Morna D (1997) *Beginnings*, London: SCM Press.

Chapter 10
The End and the Beginning

The arrest and trial

Chapter 18 marks a significant change of style. Once again, the clear narrative emerges in good writing. There are those who suggest that even here there is allegory and an attempt to use material from the scriptures to create the narrative. I reject this. This is the clear, crisp, neat narrative style that is John's Gospel at its best.

We learn that the garden across the Kedron ravine was a place that Jesus frequented with his disciples. Mark and Matthew tell us that they went to a place called Gethsemane, but there is no indication of this being a frequent haunt or where it was. On the other hand, Luke talks of them going 'as usual' to the Mount of Olives that is across the Kedron valley from the Old City of Jerusalem. Tradition has placed Gethsemane in this area because of what is said in Luke and John.

The description contains the details of the way the arresting force was equipped. It was, of course, dark. It would have been quite easy to hide in the darkness or slip away; presumably what the disciples eventually did. Judas' inside knowledge of the place and who they were looking for was an important element in their plan. They presumably had not counted on Jesus going up to them and revealing his identity.

There is no traitor's kiss in this Gospel. But all the Gospels include the incident whereby one of the high priest's servants was struck with a sword and his ear cut off. Only in this Gospel are we told that it was Peter who did this and also the name of the victim. This incident raises so many questions. Did Peter normally go around with a sword? Was this normal for a Galilean fisherman? Was it a sword as we understand it or a large knife? Had Peter armed himself because he perceived a crisis coming? One wonders why the disciples were not arrested, or at least Peter. The situation must have been one of considerable chaos. The other Gospels do not identify the follower with a sword. The idea of one of Jesus' closest followers being armed in this way seems very surprising, and the dark chaotic confusing scene in the garden gives us a less than clear picture of what really happened.

What is clear is that Jesus comes forward and makes no attempt to escape. In fact, he identifies himself with some emphasis and directs attention to himself rather than his followers. For those who were there, that must have been a very emotionally significant experience.

On to the stage comes an unnamed disciple who has access to the High Priest's residence. Does the anonymity reflect the fact that it might still be dangerous to reveal his identity? The details of how Peter got in are clearly and precisely given.

We are given a fairly detailed and vivid account of the interview of Jesus by the High Priest. The narrative is not clear about who this was, for although the Gospel says that he was taken first to Annas and then to Caiaphas, the texts themselves differ as to when the move occurred. And so one version would seem to have the conversation was between Annas and Jesus, in which case he was not actually the High Priest. The other version has it that Jesus had been moved to Caiaphas and so the interrogation was with him. Whatever did happen, it was presumably a procedure of very doubtful legality, conducted at night partly for speed and partly as it might not stand up to careful scrutiny.

Peter's denial is described in some detail with the wording of the questions. Is the source Peter himself and did he hear the interview or is it perhaps the unnamed disciple who has given this account?

John consistently has the Jewish leaders not entering Pilate's residence because they wanted to eat the Passover meal. John is quite consistent and adamant that the Passover this year was on the Sabbath.

Just as we have had a detailed account of the interview with Caiaphas so there is also a detailed account of the conversation with Pilate. Was the conversation with Pilate in Greek? Jesus probably could speak and read Greek.

Jesus is challenged about the title King of the Jews. The question put by Pilate, "Are you the King of the Jews?" is recorded in all four Gospels. But in this Gospel, it represents one of the key themes of the Gospel; just who is Jesus? Jesus is careful not to adopt the title. He neatly turns the question back to Pilate; is it his idea or something others have given him. Jesus makes it clear that he is not a king in any sense that Pilate is familiar with, and when again challenged about being a king refuses to acknowledge the word, "King is your word." John 18:37)

The details of the trial have Pilate making several attempts to release Jesus but failing. He does not come across as a very authoritative character. Firstly, he attempts to have Jesus released as a goodwill gesture for the Passover but the crowd want Barabbas. Pilate has Jesus flogged; not the action of someone who was genuinely trying to help Jesus.

The purple robe and crown of thorns are poignantly introduced. Once again, Pilate suggests releasing him but is then frightened by hearing of the claim that he might be the son of God. Jesus' words suggesting a higher authority clearly affect Pilate, and John says Pilate then tried hard to release him. However, finally the threat of the emperor is brought into play by the Jewish leaders, and this weak man finally gives in and allows Jesus to be crucified.

The detail of 'The Pavement' (John 19:14) is something which just sounds authentic. It is a typical example of the geographic and incidental detail which is characteristic of John. John gives the Jewish name and also that of the place of crucifixion. John's Gospel is clearly written for people unfamiliar with Jerusalem and Aramaic, people who saw themselves as other than Jews.

The Crucifixion

Since one of John's main themes is the identity of Jesus, it is appropriate that John includes the episode of the argument about what should be put as a label on the cross. (John 19:19–22) There is no comment on Pilate's motives. On the one hand, he could be trying to offend the Jews and demonstrate that Rome has the power to crucify their king if it chooses or it may be that he is demonstrating some sense of the importance of Jesus. The writer probably did not know and we are left to take the facts for what they are.

John tells us that Jesus, carrying his cross, 'went out to the place of the Skull' (John 19.17). That is to say that the place of execution was outside the city walls. Mark says the soldiers took Jesus out (Mark 15:21), but in the brief style of Mark it is not clear whether this is out of the Governor's quarters or the city. John tells us that the place of burial was close to the site of execution (John 19:42) and so also outside the city which is where one would expect to find burial grounds. These are small details that are consistent with John's detailed knowledge of the events.

The account of what happened to his clothing is seen as ironic in terms of the words of Psalm 22. The writer draws attention to it (John 19.24). There is no reason to suggest he invented it to make it fit the psalm. Indeed, Robinson points out that the detail of the clothing being divided into four corresponds with the fact that such assignments were regularly conducted by a group of four soldiers, a quaternion. Robinson cites various historical sources as confirmation of this[1]. It is a little detail, typical of John which is there simply as part of the narrative and demonstrates his knowledge.

What follows is a particularly moving scene where the dying Jesus entrusts the care of his mother to his close friend and likewise his care to his mother—a scene of great significance in this Gospel because it directly involves the 'disciple whom he loved' (John 19.25-27). This moment emphasises the special relationship that this disciple had with Jesus and so it is understandable that this disciple should be held in particular respect and regard by the fledgling church and is known by this special designation rather than his name.

There is, I contend, no reason to think that it is anyone other than John, the son of Zebedee.

There is little more detail about what happened on the cross apart from the drink of sour wine and that Jesus says, "It is accomplished," before dying. It is, of course, only in this Gospel that the Jews are seen asking for the removal of the bodies before the Passover as in the other Gospels Passover has already occurred. John alone gives the account of the piercing of the side with a spear.

What is curious is the witness account of this. All the Gospels are eager to make it clear that the death of Jesus on the cross was witnessed. In the light of the church's subsequent claim that Jesus had risen from the dead, it was important to make clear that he had actually died and not, as has often been suggested, that he merely was in a coma or some such condition. The witness is not identified. It suggests that the beloved disciple, John, and the women had departed. It is not clearly stated that they were present at the moment of death, but if they were, it would be quite natural that they left as soon as it was evident that he had died. Indeed, they would have wanted to make arrangements for his burial.

John tells us that the piercing was witnessed by 'an eyewitness, whose evidence is to be trusted. He knows that he speaks the truth, so that you too may believe' (John 19:35). Why are we not given the identity of this person? It would be an odd way to refer to the beloved disciple who elsewhere is identified as authenticating the Gospel. One can conjecture that the disciple who helped Peter into the High Priest's courtyard was in a position of danger but simply to have been present at this action seems uncontroversial.

The details of his burial are interesting. Firstly, that Nicodemus makes another appearance. All four Gospels explain that Joseph of Arimathea took the body and put it into a tomb. Presumably, he was someone of considerable status and repute. The account wants to make it clear that Jesus' body was laid in the tomb and done so by this trustworthy citizen; an important fact to establish since the body is no longer there and the Gospel writers are proclaiming the resurrection.

Much has been made of the amount of spices that they brought to the burial. Robinson goes into detail to explain that the quantity is not as large as some have supposed and furthermore that what was happening was that the body was being preserved as well as possible over the Sabbath when the final appropriate steps could be taken.[2]

The Resurrection

The resurrection stories are very special parts of the Gospel. They are told with a simple elegance. There is no commentary apart from the final words of Jesus at the end of the third account. There are three resurrection stories apart from the epilogue: the two disciples who run to the tomb, Mary Magdalene's encounter, and the story of Thomas which is itself in two parts.

The first account is that of the beloved disciple. This is told in detail: a very personal and detailed account from the person who is the source of the Gospel. It starts with the simple discovery by Mary Magdalene that the tomb is empty, and she makes the very sensible and obvious response, "They have taken the Lord out of his tomb." The story is filled with urgency as she runs to Peter and the beloved disciple. It makes sense that she would go to Peter and John, two of the inner group of the disciples.

Peter and the other disciple run to the tomb. I believe that what follows is the description of the few moments when the evangelist came to faith through the resurrection. The momentous few minutes are described as the point of climax is reached. John arrives at the tomb first but does not enter. The grave clothes are still in the tomb; not removed with the body, nor cast aside, as one would expect a grave robber to do, but placed purposely. The findings are taken in, but this is not yet the moment that changes everything. Then he enters the tomb, and that is the exact moment it all clicked. Here are the all-important words, 'he saw and believed.' This is the core of the Gospel; the writer wants everybody to see and believe.

That this is a very personal account is highlighted by the fact that we are not told what Peter's reaction was. What did he at that moment think and believe? The only comment or description of how Peter reacted is that we are told that, 'until then they had not understood the scriptures, which shows that he must rise from the dead' (John 20:9). John's understanding is apparently shared with Peter. We are told simply that they went home again. This is a deeply personal religious experience from the perspective of the individual for whom it was the turning point of his life.

The second testimony, that of Mary of Magdala, follows. It is evident that whatever had happened to John had made no impact on Mary. She is still weeping and still believing that someone has removed the body. Understandably, on being aware of someone whom she presumes is a gardener, she tries to solve the mystery of the missing body. She too describes in detail the moment when she suddenly believed that Jesus was risen. Whereas for John it had been entering the empty tomb, for her it was hearing her name said by Jesus.

There is no instruction about going to Galilee which is there in Mark and Matthew and definitely not in Luke. As mentioned earlier, this is a matter of difference between the clear message in Mark and Matthew and the instruction in Luke to stay in Jerusalem.

John's Gospel seems confused on this point. The message Mary conveys is not about going to Galilee or about staying but the promise of ascension. Of course the story then goes on with the disciples receiving the Spirit and, in the epilogue, they go to Galilee, or at least some of them do.

The third resurrection story then is that of Thomas. Jesus appears to the disciples when they were behind locked doors and when Thomas was absent. This appearance includes the gift of the Spirit and words of commission, "As the Father sent me, so I send you" (John 20:21). The story then moves on to describe Thomas' lack of belief and the subsequent appearance a week later. There is no suggestion as to what the disciples had been doing in this week. They still felt the need of locked doors it seems. Thomas' response on seeing Jesus contains a great affirmation of faith. Whereas the other appearances have not produced any statement on the part of the witnesses, Thomas asserts that Jesus is "My Lord and my God" (John 20:28). At the climatic conclusion of the Gospel is this great assertion about Jesus.

The crucial message for everyone is the message, "Happy are they who never saw me and yet have found faith." This is what the book is for; this what the writer is urging others to do, have faith.

These few simple sentences mark the end of the chapter as we know it and surely must have been originally the end of the book. 'There was a lot more that could be said about what Jesus did but what is written here is written so that you may hold the faith that Jesus is the Christ, the Son of God and that through this faith you may possess eternal life by his name.' One can almost see, 'The End' following. Just as the book has had a magnificent opening this is the great finale. Yet we have more, by apparently the same author.

The epilogue

This final part of the Gospel tells of a resurrection appearance in Galilee. This story throws up as many questions as any in the Gospel. What were the disciples doing fishing if they had received the Holy Spirit? Unlike a lot of the Gospel the timing is vague, 'Sometime later...'

The story has lots of detail with the charcoal fire and the way the catch was made: the enthusiastic Peter whose character is so well-revealed in the Synoptic Gospels plunging into the sea to get to shore quickly. It fits with everything else we know of this person.

It is difficult to know what to make of the number of fish. This has been a source of speculation by commentators. If it has some significance for the early church, it is fairly obscure. It is perhaps a detail remembered and has no other significance but that will not stop people suggesting it has an allegorical meaning.

The detail of the disciples not daring to ask, 'Who are you?' (John 21:12) is so typical of the realistic touch of the Gospel. The awkward feelings of the disciples and how they reacted is a vivid image of human nature.

There is a sense of an ending to the story with the words, 'This makes the third time that Jesus appeared to his disciples after his resurrection from the dead' (John 21:14). Incidentally, in saying this, it would seem to correlate with the appearance to two disciples as described in Luke's description of the two journeying to Emmaus and the assertion of Paul that Jesus appeared to Peter, 'he appeared to Cephas and afterwards to the twelve' (1 Cor 15:5) which is corroborated by Luke 24:34.

What follows is the famous dialogue between Jesus and Peter which has a standing of its own. Its importance appears to be that it confers the authority of leading the church on Peter despite his denial of Jesus and also the explanation that the expectation that Jesus would return before the beloved disciple died was not explicitly promised by Jesus.

The conversation itself is something of a mystery. It relies on the subtleties of Greek in that different words for love are used. But this is a carpenter from Nazareth talking to a fisherman from Capernaum. Why are they talking in Greek? The first two times Jesus asks Peter if he loves him, a form of the word, '*agape*' is used. Peter responds using a different word, '*philo*'. The third time Jesus uses this word which hurts Peter. If they were talking in Aramaic, as one might expect, then these words do not exist. There is a possibility that one used the Aramaic word which is normally translated as love but the other used the word associated with friendship. Perhaps they were talking in Greek. In any case, it is not clear just what the significance is between '*philo*' and '*agape*' for each of them. It is one more mystery about the Gospel for which we can have no certain solution.

There is then what presumably is an important passage for the church about John. It is not unreasonable to suggest that this whole section was added after John had died. People had believed he would live to see the second coming. Care is being taken to state that this was never promised.

Finally we are given an assurance that it is this disciple's testimony which is being recorded. There follows a contradictory sentence. It says that John wrote it and 'we know that his testimony is true.' Clearly, he did not write that sentence. Who is the 'we' and what do they mean when they say he wrote it. The last words that we have suddenly switch to the first person singular, 'I suppose the whole world could not hold the books that would be written.' (John 21:25) Who is this individual? There is something ironic in the teasing way this Gospel finally ends.

References

1. Robinson, John A T (1985) *The Priority of John*, London: SCM Press, p178.
2. Ibid p282–283

Conclusion

There are many books about John's Gospel, some works of great scholarship and erudition. Throughout history, great minds have applied years of learning, study and expertise to the Gospel. The book itself is of a very different nature. John's Gospel is a work of passion, enthusiasm and in every sense of the word, evangelical. The purpose of the book is clearly stated. Without any compromise, the book is written to bring people to have faith in Jesus as the Christ and in so doing to attain the greatest prize of all, life linked to God which is thereby eternal. This is no modest or minor undertaking, but then again as one considers its impact in the many centuries since it was written, it is evident that it has achieved its purpose many, many times.

I have suggested that the book is what it claims to be, the testimony of a disciple who was particularly close to Jesus and given the title of 'the disciple whom Jesus loved'. Furthermore, I believe there are good reasons for maintaining that this person is John, the son of Zebedee. The witness is therefore someone who was not only a close friend but present at most of the important events of the Gospel.

His account is therefore likely to be built around historical details that are as reliable as and quite possibly more reliable than the sources that are behind the Synoptics. Far from assuming that when John differs from the Synoptics in detail it is John that has altered things for some ulterior motive, rather we should question the accuracy of the synoptic account.

John's Gospel is at times complicated in its structure and the story keeps jumping from place to place and time to time. This I maintain is more proof of its authenticity than reason to doubt it and it is, I suggest, not difficult to consider that the Synoptics have tidied up the story to make a more elegant and, in some ways, more dramatic account.

John's account contains some of the most profound, powerful and commanding of statements and descriptions, but it also contains repetition both in that the same thing is said twice but also that a subject is revisited. The contrast between the quality of the writing on one hand and the quality of the literary organisation on the other is at the heart of the great debates about the Gospel. A highly plausible explanation is that the author is not John himself but someone who is recording John's teaching.

Thus there is created a blurred distinction between what John saw and heard Jesus say and do, and what is his interpretation and explanation, part of his teaching. Furthermore, it is quite possible that as someone very close to Jesus, living with him for three years, John himself may be uncertain as to what exactly he heard uttered and what he came to understand. John describes how his understanding increased on entering the empty tomb (John 20:9). If the Gospel is the testimony of the apostle John, then his own development in faith and understanding is at the heart of the book.

If we wish to take John's Gospel in the context of a shared Christian faith, then we should believe that the Holy Spirit has played a crucial part in its construction. To believe that the Gospel writers were inspired by the Holy Spirit is not to believe that they were incapable of making a mistake. We believe the church has been led by the Spirit but it has made many mistakes throughout its history from St Peter, as Paul points out (Gal 2:11–12), to the present day. On the other hand, there is no reason to think that the Gospel's avowed aim of bringing people to faith, is not Spirit-inspired and that it has been true to the message. There is no reason to think that there is some deviant theology, invented narrative or encrypted subtext. The Gospel is what it claims to be and coming as it does from the disciple whom Jesus loved, it is perhaps as close to Jesus as anything that is written.

We now understand that our whole earth is one of several planets circulating around one star in a vast galaxy which in itself is one of a multitude that make up the universe. Consequently, in this context, anything that happens in our world is of no significance. Yet, of course, we live our lives not on that basis, but with the perspective that our world is what matters.

I suggest that we can see something analogous in the way we look at the New Testament and John's Gospel in particular. If we view the Gospel as simply one of the myriads of books that have been written and that the events are just details about a handful of people amongst the billions who have ever lived then these writings are unimportant. However, we are invited to consider this book to be of supreme importance for everyone. The Gospel was written so that people might have faith, but it is ironically faith itself which gives significance and authority to the words. Do we trust John's Gospel? Does it reveal the Word of God, that is to say the Word made flesh? That is the decision we all have to make for ourselves.